WOMEN'S ISSUES

COMBAT SERVICE OPPORTUNITIES FOR WOMEN

EXPANSION AND PROGRESS ISSUES

WOMEN'S ISSUES

Additional books in this series can be found on Nova's website under the Series tab.

Additional e-books in this series can be found on Nova's website under the e-book tab.

WOMEN'S ISSUES

COMBAT SERVICE OPPORTUNITIES FOR WOMEN

EXPANSION AND PROGRESS ISSUES

CASSANDRA SCHULTZ
EDITOR

nova publishers
New York

NOTICE TO THE READER

The Publisher has taken reasonable care in the preparation of this book, but makes no expressed or implied warranty of any kind and assumes no responsibility for any errors or omissions. No liability is assumed for incidental or consequential damages in connection with or arising out of information contained in this book. The Publisher shall not be liable for any special, consequential, or exemplary damages resulting, in whole or in part, from the readers' use of, or reliance upon, this material. Any parts of this book based on government reports are so indicated and copyright is claimed for those parts to the extent applicable to compilations of such works.

Independent verification should be sought for any data, advice or recommendations contained in this book. In addition, no responsibility is assumed by the publisher for any injury and/or damage to persons or property arising from any methods, products, instructions, ideas or otherwise contained in this publication.

This publication is designed to provide accurate and authoritative information with regard to the subject matter covered herein. It is sold with the clear understanding that the Publisher is not engaged in rendering legal or any other professional services. If legal or any other expert assistance is required, the services of a competent person should be sought. FROM A DECLARATION OF PARTICIPANTS JOINTLY ADOPTED BY A COMMITTEE OF THE AMERICAN BAR ASSOCIATION AND A COMMITTEE OF PUBLISHERS.

Additional color graphics may be available in the e-book version of this book.

Library of Congress Cataloging-in-Publication Data

ISBN: 978-1-63484-432-1

Published by Nova Science Publishers, Inc. † New York

CONTENTS

Preface		**vii**
Chapter 1	Women in Combat: Issues for Congress *Kristy N. Kamarck*	**1**
Chapter 2	Military Personnel: DOD Is Expanding Combat Service Opportunities for Women, but Should Monitor Long-Term Integration Progress *United States Government Accountability Office*	**35**
Chapter 3	Memorandum re: Women in the Service Implementation Plan *General Martin E. Dempsey*	**87**
Chapter 4	Memorandum re: Elimination of the 1994 Direct Ground Combat Definition and Assignment Rule *General Martin E. Dempsey and Leon E. Panetta*	**91**
Index		**95**

PREFACE

Over the past two decades of conflict, women have served with valor and continue to serve on combat aircraft, naval vessels, and in support of ground combat operations. The expansion of roles for women in the armed forces has evolved since the early days of the military when women were restricted by law and policy from serving in certain occupations and units. Women are not precluded by law from serving in any military unit or occupational specialty. However, a 1994 Department of Defense (DOD) policy prevented women from being assigned to units below brigade level where the unit's primary mission was to engage directly in ground combat. This policy barred women from serving in infantry, artillery, armor, combat engineers, and special operations units of battalion size or smaller. On January 24, 2013, then-Secretary of Defense Leon Panetta rescinded the rule that restricted women from serving in combat units and directed the military departments to review their occupational standards and assignment policies for implementation no later than January 1, 2016. This book reviews the issues for Congress of having women in combat. It also assesses the status of service efforts to open positions and occupations to women, including steps to identify and mitigate potential challenges; extent the services' efforts to validate gender-neutral occupational standards are consistent with statutory and Joint Staff requirements; and extent DOD is tracking, monitoring, and providing oversight of the services' integration plans.

In: Combat Service Opportunities for Women ISBN: 978-1-63484-432-1
Editor: Cassandra Schultz

Chapter 1

WOMEN IN COMBAT: ISSUES FOR CONGRESS*

Kristy N. Kamarck

SUMMARY

Over the past two decades of conflict, women have served with valor and continue to serve on combat aircraft, naval vessels, and in support of ground combat operations. The expansion of roles for women in the armed forces has evolved since the early days of the military when women were restricted by law and policy from serving in certain occupations and units. Women are not precluded by law from serving in any military unit or occupational specialty. However, a 1994 Department of Defense (DOD) policy prevented women from being assigned to units below brigade level where the unit's primary mission was to engage directly in ground combat. This policy barred women from serving in infantry, artillery, armor, combat engineers, and special operations units of battalion size or smaller. On January 24, 2013, then-Secretary of Defense Leon Panetta rescinded the rule that restricted women from serving in combat units and directed the military departments to review their occupational standards and assignment policies for implementation no later than January 1, 2016.

This recent policy change followed extensive reviews by various commissions and others on issues regarding women in the military and

* This is an edited, reformatted and augmented version of a Congressional Research Service publication, No. R42075, dated September 1, 2015.

policies for their assignment and career progression. For example, the Duncan Hunter National Defense Authorization Act for Fiscal Year 2009 (P.L. 110-417) established the Military Leadership Diversity Commission whose mandate was to conduct a study and report on the "establishment and maintenance of fair promotion and command opportunities for ethnic- and gender-specific members of the Armed Forces." Among its recommendations, the commission stated that DOD should take deliberate steps to open additional career fields and units involved in direct ground combat to women. The commission's recommendations prompted Congress to direct DOD, in the Ike Skelton National Defense Act for Fiscal Year 2011 (P.L. 111-383), to conduct a review to "ensure that female members have equitable opportunities to compete and excel in the Armed Forces."

With the cancellation of the policy banning women from serving in combat units, some have questioned whether current occupational standards for entry into these units should be kept in place or modified. Proponents of change maintain that the existing standards are artificially high, and act as a de facto exclusionary barrier to the entry of women into combat occupations. Defenders of the current standards view any reductions to the existing standards as potentially damaging to military readiness.

Congress has established requirements, definitions, and criteria for the development and application of "gender-neutral" occupational standards, and has oversight of all DOD decisions in this matter. Congress may also consider additional issues including equal opportunity, equal responsibility (such as selective service registration), readiness and cohesion, effectiveness, and the overall manpower needs of the military.

ISSUE

Laws prohibiting women from serving in air and naval combat units were repealed in the early 1990s. However, until recently, it has been Department of Defense (DOD) policy to restrict women from certain combat-related units and military occupations, especially ground combat units. Despite the official policies barring women from ground combat positions, many female servicemembers have served in combat environments for much of the recent history of the U.S. military. In the past two decades of conflict in Iraq and Afghanistan, the lines between combat and noncombat roles have become increasingly blurred and as a result DOD's exclusion policies have been called into question. As of April 2015, 161 women have lost their lives and 1,015 had been wounded in action as part of Global War on Terror (GWOT) operations (See Table 1).[1] In addition, in modern combat operations, over 9,000 women have received Army Combat Action Badges for "actively engaging or being engaged by the enemy," and two have received Silver Stars for "gallantry in action against an enemy of the United States."[2]

Table 1. Female Casualties in the Global War on Terror April 2015

Female Deaths					
Operation	Army	Navy	Marine Corps	Air Force	Total
OEF	36	5	2	8	51
OIF	89	10	8	3	110
OND	0	0	0	0	0
Total	125	15	10	11	161
Females Wounded in Action					
Wounded in Action	Army	Navy	Marine Corps	Air Force	Total
OEF	314	5	29	28	376
OIF	547	6	41	33	627
OND	11	0	0	1	12
Total	872	11	70	62	1,015

Source: Defense Manpower Data Center (DMDC) Defense Casualty Analysis System.

Notes: OEF (Operation Enduring Freedom), OIF (Operation Iraqi Freedom), OND (Operation New Dawn).

On January 24, 2013, the Secretary of Defense rescinded all ground combat restrictions for women and directed the military departments to implement the new policy no later than January 1, 2016.[3] For DOD, implementation may require adjustments to recruiting, assignment, physical standards, and other personnel policies. As directed by the Secretary of Defense, the military departments have been conducting a series of reviews and studies to assess what changes or exceptions may need prior to the implementation deadline.[4]

Those in favor of keeping restrictions cite physiological differences between men and women that could potentially affect military readiness and unit effectiveness. Some also argue that social and cultural barriers exist to the successful integration of women into combat occupations and all-male units.

Those who advocate for opening all military occupations to women emphasize equal rights and argue it is more difficult for servicemembers to advance to top-ranking positions in the armed services without combat experience. In their view, modern weapons have equalized the potential for women in combat since wars are less likely to be fought on a hand-to-hand basis. In this regard, properly trained women would be able to perform successfully in combat and exempting them from serving in combat is unfair to men.

The military departments are required by law (10 U.S.C. §652) to notify Congress of changes that would alter occupational standards or open any new military career designators to women. Congress then has a 30-day (continuous in-session) review period upon receiving notification of the changes before DOD can implement them. Congress has authority to make changes in these matters and may consider additional issues including equal opportunity, equal responsibility (such as selective service registration), readiness and cohesion, and the overall manpower needs of the military.[5]

Background

While DOD policy has only recently opened combat roles to female servicemembers, women have been recognized for military service in combat since the American Revolutionary War. In 1776, Margaret Cochran Corbin became the first woman to receive a military pension from Congress for an injury sustained while helping to defend Fort Washington against British troops.[6] However, for most of the history of the U.S. military, women's roles were primarily clerical in nature or in support of military medical services. Women did not serve formally in the military until Congress established the Army Nurse Corps as a permanent organization within the Medical Department under the Army Reorganization Act of 1901.[7] In 1908 Congress enacted language which led to the creation of the Navy Nurse Corps.[8]

World War II and the Women's Armed Services Integration Act

In the earlier part of the twentieth century, the idea of enlisting women into the armed services was met with broad opposition from military commanders, Congress, and the public. However, the upsurge in manpower needs of World War II compelled Congress to open more service roles to women. In 1942, Congress opened the Naval Reserve to women[9] and also created the Women's Army Auxiliary Corps for the purpose of

> noncombatant service with the Army of the United States for the purpose of making available to the national defense when needed the knowledge, skill, and special training of the women of this Nation.[10]

In 1943, Congress established the Marine Corps Women's Reserve and made the Women's Army Corps (WAC) a part of the regular Army on a temporary basis.[11] By the end of the war nearly 400,000 women had served in armed services as members of the Army and Navy Nurse Corps, Women's Army Corps (WAC), Navy (WAVES), Coast Guard (SPARs) and Marine Corps Women's Reserves or with partner organizations like the American Red Cross, the United Services Organization (USO), and the Civil Air Patrol.[12] Approximately 543 military women died in the line of duty during World War II and 84 others were held as prisoners of war (POWs).[13]

Following World War II, Congress made women a permanent part of the military through the Women's Armed Services Integration Act of 1948.[14] This legislation included two exclusionary statutes prohibiting assignment of female members to duty in aircraft engaged in combat and to vessels engaged in, or likely to be engaged in combat missions.[15] The legislation also limited the proportion of women in the military to 2% of the enlisted force and 10% of officers.

The All-Volunteer Force and Social Change

In the 1960s and 1970s, two major factors led to the expansion of the role of women in the armed forces. First, after the end of the draft and the beginning of the All-Volunteer Force in December 1973, the armed services had difficulty in recruiting and retaining enough qualified males, thereby turning attention to recruiting women.[16] Second, the movement for equal rights for women led to demands for equal opportunity in all occupational fields, including national defense.

The limit on the percentage of women in the military was eventually repealed in 1967 and the number of women serving continued to grow through the next three decades.[17] While the number of women in the military increased, various pieces of legislation in the 1970s also broadened the opportunities for female servicemembers. In 1974, the age requirement for women enlisting without parental consent was made the same as for men.[18] In the next year, legislation was enacted that allowed women to be admitted to the three service academies, and the first women were admitted in the summer of 1976.[19] In 1977, Congress directed the Secretary of Defense to submit to Congress a definition of the term "combat" and recommendations for expanding job classifications for female members of the armed forces.[20] By 1978, women were permitted to be assigned permanent duty on noncombatant Navy ships, and up to six months of temporary duty on other ships.[21]

As women became more integrated into the military, the question was raised as to whether women should be required to register for the Selective Service. In 1979, when considering the reinstitution of Selective Service registration, the Senate Armed Services Committee cited legal and policy restrictions on women in combat as one of the reasons for differential treatment of men and women by Selective Service. In addition, the committee stated

> The committee feels strongly that it is not in the best interest of our national defense to register women for the Military Selective Service Act, which would provide needed military personnel upon mobilization or in the event of a peacetime draft for the armed forces.[22]

As the percentage of women in service increased and they became more integrated into units serving in combat zones, there was a general lack of clarity on what role women could play in support of combat units and combat operations. One early example of this was during Operation Urgent Fury on October 25, 1983 when U.S. service personnel were sent for an evacuation of noncombatant American citizens on the island nation of Grenada. Four U.S. military police women arrived in Grenada shortly after the invasion and were promptly sent back to Fort Bragg, N.C.[23] At Fort Bragg, Major General Edward Trobaugh, then-commander of the 82nd Airborne Division had removed all the females from the invasion Task Force. Following an intervention by Lieutenant General Jack Mackmull, then-commander of XVIII Airborne Corps, women were reattached to the unit and finally deployed to Barbados on November 2, 1983, to serve with the lead element of the Task Force while the rest of the Task Force deployed to Grenada the same day.[24]

The "Risk Rule" for Assignment of Women

In January 1988, the Department of Defense Task Force on Women in the Military noted that the varying definitions of a "combat mission" had led to inconsistencies between the military departments in the assignment of women.[25] In response to the task force findings, DOD adopted a "risk rule" that excluded women from noncombat units or missions if the risks of exposure to direct combat, hostile fire, or capture were equal to or greater than the risks in the combat units they support. In this regard, the policy prohibited the colocation of women with combat units. For example, a female medic could be assigned to a noncombat support unit; however, if that unit was called on to provided support to a combat unit, the risk to the medical support unit would have to be less than the risk to the combat unit for the female servicemember to be assigned.

Also in 1988, the General Accounting Office (now the Government Accountability Office, GAO) noted a primary barrier to the expansion of the number of women in the armed services was that women were not allowed in most combat jobs, and were also barred from many combat-related jobs.[26] The GAO reported approximately 15% of active duty positions were closed to women. Of the closed positions 41% were closed due to the risk rule's collocation policy and 46% were classified as direct ground combat positions.[27] The GAO's report also noted that the primary rationale for excluding women from direct ground combat occupations included, lack of public and congressional support, lack of support by servicewomen, and lack of need given that there were an adequate number of men available to fill those positions.

During Operations Desert Shield/Desert Storm in Iraq and Kuwait, women played a more prominent role than in previous conflicts. Approximately 16 women were killed during the conflict and two women were taken prisoner, becoming the first female POWs since World War II.[28] Then-Major Rhonda Cornum, an Army flight surgeon, was captured when her helicopter was shot down during a search and rescue mission. During her captivity, she was sexually assaulted, which again raised public concern about the roles of women in combat and the risks that they faced.[29]

Following Operation Desert Storm, efforts to expand the assignment of women were renewed by civil rights and women's advocacy groups. Legislation enacted in 1991 called for the repeal of the statutory limitations on the assignment of women in the armed forces to combat aircraft and naval vessels and the establishment of a Presidential Commission on the Assignment of Women in the Armed Forces.[30] On November 15, 1992, the commission issued its report. Some key recommendations were the following:

- DOD should establish a policy to ensure that no person who is best qualified is denied access on the basis of gender to an assignment that is open to both men and women. As far as it is compatible with the above policy, the Secretary of Defense should retain discretion to set goals that encourage the recruitment and optimize the utilization of women in the armed services, allowing for the requirements of each military department.

- Military readiness should be the driving concern regarding assignment policies; there are circumstances under which women might be assigned to combat positions.
- Women should be excluded from direct land combat units and positions. Furthermore the commission recommends that the existing service policies concerning direct land combat exclusion be codified. Service Secretaries shall recommend to the Congress which units and positions should fall under the land combat exclusions.
- Current DOD and Service policies with regard to Army, Air Force and Navy aircraft on combat missions should be retained and codified by means of the reenactment of Section 8549 of Title 10, U.S. Code which was repealed by P.L. 102-190, Section 531 for the Air Force, and reenactment of the provisions of 10 U.S.C. Section 6015 prohibiting women from assignment to duty on aircraft engaged in combat missions, which was repealed by P.L. 102-190 for the Navy, and codification of Army policy.
- Existing laws and Service policies prohibiting servicewomen from service on combatant vessels should be repealed or modified, except for those applying to submarines and amphibious vessels.
- DOD should retain the risk rule [as explained above] as currently implemented. Navy policies which implement the risk rule should be modified to reflect the changes made [in the above recommendation].[31]

In addition, the commission recommended retaining the current policies prohibiting the assignment of women in special operations forces.[32]

Repeal of the "Risk Rule" and a New Direct Ground Combat Definition and Assignment Rule

On April 28, 1993, then-Secretary of Defense Les Aspin released a memorandum directing the military departments to open more positions to women and establishing an implementation committee to review and make recommendations on such implementation issues.

Several months later, as part of the National Defense Authorization Act for FY1994 (P.L. 103 160), Congress enacted language that

- repealed the prohibition on women serving on combatant vessels and aircraft,
- required the Secretary of Defense to ensure occupational performance standards were gender-neutral, and
- required the Secretary of Defense to notify the House and Senate Armed Services Committees 90 days before any policy changes were to be made concerning the assignment of women to ground combat roles, and, required the Secretary of Defense to notify these committees 30 days prior to the opening of any "combatant unit, class of combatant vessel, or type of combat platform" to women.[33]

In 1994, Secretary Aspin officially rescinded the "risk rule" and approved a new Direct Ground Combat and Assignment Rule, sometimes called the Direct Combat Exclusion Rule:

> **A. Rule.** Service members are eligible to be assigned to all positions for which they are qualified, except that women shall be excluded from assignment to units below the brigade[34] level whose primary mission is to engage in direct combat on the ground, as defined below.
>
> **B. Definition.** Direct ground combat is engaging an enemy on the ground with individual or crew served weapons, while being exposed to hostile fire and to a high probability of direct physical contact with the hostile force's personnel. Direct ground combat takes place well forward on the battlefield while locating and closing with the enemy to defeat them by fire, maneuver, or shock effect.[35]

Secretary Aspin further specified that these assignment policies and regulations may include restrictions on the assignment of women:

- where the Service Secretary attests that the cost of appropriate berthing and privacy arrangements are prohibitive;
- where units and positions doctrinally required to physically collocate and remain with direct combat units that are closed to women;
- where units are engaged in long range reconnaissance operations and Special Operations Forces missions; and

- where job related physical requirements would necessarily exclude the vast majority of women Servicemembers.[36]

Supporters of these changes noted that they would open more opportunities for women in the armed services. Critics saw these changes as putting women at greater risk since they removed the "substantial risk" of being captured from the definition of ground combat.

Women in Combat Zones: Iraq and Afghanistan

In the first decade of the 21st century, several situations evolved that highlighted the disparity between the policy prohibiting women from assignment to direct ground combat units and the roles actually performed by women. Operation Enduring Freedom (OEF) in 2001 and Operation Iraqi Freedom (OIF) in 2003 were the first large-scale mobilizations of U.S. troops since Operation Desert Shield/Desert Storm in the early 1990s. The nonlinear battlefields of Iraq and Afghanistan blurred the distinctions between forward and rear operating areas, often placing support units in the proximity of active engagements. The public debate over the assignment of women was reinvigorated when three Army women were captured by enemy forces in Iraq and sustained injuries following the ambush of their unit.[37] The women were assigned to Army's 507th Maintenance Company which provided logistic support to ground units, and thus not a unit whose primary mission was to engage in direct combat on the ground.

Also, in 2005 the Army started moving towards a "Modular Redesign" for rotation, training, and readiness reasons.[38] Under this concept, the Brigade Combat Teams (BCTs) served as the basic large tactical combat unit of the Army. These BCTs were supported by Multi-Functional Support Brigades. These support brigades were often collocated with the BCTs included noncombat personnel, many of whom were women. Such collocation appeared to some to be at odds with the 1994 policies on the assignment of women.

Because of the nonlinear and irregular nature of the battle in Iraq and Afghanistan, the definition of "direct ground combat" in the 1994 policy became less useful: what did "well forward" mean on a nonlinear battlefield, and how useful was the "primary mission" criteria when noncombat units regularly engage in direct combat to carry out their mission? In this environment, the Army and Marine Corps utilized women to search Iraqi females for weapons, and to patrol with foot soldiers, usually in door-to-door-type operations.[39] Also, women were increasingly involved in convoy escort missions that came under fire[40] and were embedded with special operations forces (SOF) in Cultural Support Teams that helped units deal with local Afghani females while operating in Afghan villages.[41] In 2005, Sergeant Leigh Ann Hester, an Army soldier, became the first female soldier to be awarded the Silver Star since World War II and the first to be cited for close combat action.[42]

Concerns over the collocation and forward deployment of support units resulted in language being included in the House version of the National Defense Authorization Act for Fiscal Year 2006. Under this law, if the Secretary of Defense proposed to make any change to the 1994 ground combat exclusion policy, or open or close military career fields that had been in effect since May 18, 2005, the Secretary must first notify Congress and then wait 30 days (while Congress is in session) before implementing any such change.[43] In addition, the Secretary of Defense was directed to submit a report concerning the Secretary's review of the current and future implementation of the policy regarding the assignment of women with particular attention to the Army's unit modularization efforts and associated assignment policies.

In a 2007 report, the RAND Corporation noted while the Army was complying with the DOD assignment policy, it may not have been complying with the separate Army assignment policy.[44] Further, the report stated

> [w]e find considerable evidence that support units are collocated with direct combat units if the definition of collocation is based purely on proximity. However, if the definition of collocation is based on interdependency *and* proximity, the evidence is inconclusive.[45]

The report noted that hundreds of female Army members had received a Combat Action Badge, suggesting that the Army has recognized the combat service of women regardless of whether the women had been assigned in compliance with policy.[46] While the RAND report stopped short of recommending that more assignments be open to women, the authors did recommend that assignment policies for women be redrafted to "conform—and clarify how it conforms—to the nature of warfare today and in the future."[47]

Women on Submarines

While women have been allowed by law to serve on surface combatants in the Navy since the early 1990s, women have been barred by policy from assignments on submarines until just recently. The early arguments for not assigning women to submarine duty in were not related to the dangers of combat, but instead related to privacy and habitability issues in cramped spaces and cost concerns for retrofitting submarines to accommodate both men and women.[48] As early as 2000, based on recommendations by the Defense Advisory Committee on Women in the Services (DACOWITS), efforts were made by the Pentagon to open up assignments for women on submarines.[49] However, these recommendations met with some opposition from senior Navy officials and Members of Congress who cited cost concerns for berthing modifications, privacy concerns, the possibility of sexual misconduct affecting unit cohesion and effectiveness.[50]

As a result, language was contained in the Floyd D. Spence National Defense Authorization Act for Fiscal Year 2001 (P.L. 106-398) that seemingly halted the Pentagon's efforts. Essentially, this language prohibited the Navy from assigning women to submarines from May 10, 2000 forward until the Secretary of Defense submits to Congress written notice of such a proposed change and following a period of 30 days of "continuous session of Congress (excluding any day on which either the House of Congress is not in session)...."[51]

It was not until February 23, 2010, that Secretary of Defense Robert Gates notified Congress of a decision by the Navy to allow women to serve on nuclear submarines.[52] In 2011, the Navy began assigning female officers to submarines. In 2015 the Navy began accepting applications for assignment of enlisted women to submarines, and on June 22, 2015, announced a list of 38 female enlisted sailors that will begin training to convert to a submarine rating.[53]

Military Leadership Diversity Commission

The Duncan Hunter National Defense Authorization Act for Fiscal Year 2009[54] contained language establishing the Military Leadership Diversity Commission. Among its duties, the commission was to conduct a study and file a report regarding diversity issues in the Armed Forces with attention to the "establishment and maintenance of fair promotion and command opportunities for ethnic- and gender-specific members of the Armed Forces at the O-5[55] grade level and above." In March, 2011, the commission released its report, *From Representation to Inclusion: Diversity Leadership and the 2 1st-Century Military.*[56] Three of its recommendations were particularly relevant to the issue of women and combat.

Recommendation 9:

> DOD and the Services should eliminate the "combat exclusion policies" (discussed later in this report) for women, including the removal of barriers and inconsistencies, to create a level playing field for all qualified servicemembers. The Commission recommends a time-phased approach:
>
> - Women in career fields/specialties currently open to them should be immediately able to be assigned to any unit that requires that career field/specialty, consistent with current operational environment.
> - DOD and the Services should take deliberate steps in a phased approach to open additional career fields and units involved in "direct ground combat" to qualified women.
> - DOD and the Services should report to Congress the process and timeline for removing barriers that inhibit women from achieving senior leadership positions.

Recommendation 18:

> As part of the accountability reviews, the Services, in conjunction with the Chief Diversity Officer (established in Recommendation 15), should conduct annual "barrier analyses" to review demographic diversity patterns across the military life cycle, starting with accessions....
>
> The annual analyses should include:
>
> - accession demographics;
> - retention, command selection, and promotion rates by race/ethnicity and gender;
> - analysis of assignment patterns by race/ethnicity and gender;
> - analysis of attitudinal survey data by race/ethnicity and gender;
> - identification of persistent, group-specific deviations from overal l averages and plans to investigate underlying causes; and
> - summaries of progress made on previous actions.

Recommendation 20:

> ... Congress should revise Title 10, Section 113, to require the Secretary of Defense to report annual l y an assessment of the avai lable pool of qual ified racial/ethnic minority and female candidates for the 3- and 4-star flag/general officer positions.
>
> The Secretary of Defense must ensure that all qualified candidates (including racial/ethnic minorities and women) have been considered for nomination of every 3- and 4-star position. If there were no qualified racial/ethnic minority and/or female candidates, then a statement of explanation should be made in the package submitted to the Senate for the confirmation hearings.[57]

This last recommendation flows from the commission's finding that the combat exclusion policy limits women's opportunities to attain the highest ranks in the military. Retired Air Force General Lester L. Lyles who chaired the commission stated, "We know that [the exclusion] hinders women from promotion. [...] they're not getting credit for being in combat arms, [and] that's important for their considerations for the most senior flag ranks."[58]

DOD Review of Combat Exclusion Policies

The concern for equal opportunities for women in military leadership motivated a further review of the DOD's combat exclusion policies. Section 535 of the Ike Skelton National Defense Act for Fiscal Year 2011[59] mandated this review, stating

> (a) REVIEW REQUIRED—The Secretary of Defense, in coordination with the Secretaries of the military departments, shall conduct a review of laws, policies, and regulations, including the collocation policy,[60] that may restrict the service of female members of the Armed Forces to determine whether changes in such laws, policies, and regulations are needed to ensure that female members have equitable opportunities to compete and excel in the Armed Forces.
>
> (b) SUBMISSION OF RESULTS—Not later than April 15, 2011, the Secretary of Defense shall submit to the congressional defense committees a report containing the results of the review.

In February 2012, the Office of the Under Secretary of Defense (Personnel and Readiness) released its report. Some of the findings were that there was no indication that females had "less than equitable opportunities to compete and excel under current assignment policy," and there were "serious practical barriers" to the full elimination of gender assignment policies. The report also acknowledged that, given the nature the modern battlespace, the collocation policy had become irrelevant.[61] In the conclusion, it stated

The Department intends to:

1) Eliminate the collocation exclusion from the 1994 policy;
2) As an exception to policy, allow Military Department Secretaries to assign women in open occupational specialties to select units and positions at the battalion level (for Army, Navy, and Marine Corps) whose primary mission is to engage in direct combat on the ground;
3) Based on the exception to the policy, assess the suitability and relevance of the direct ground combat unit assignment prohibition to inform policy decisions; and
4) Pursue the development of gender-neutral physical standards for occupational specialties closed due to physical requirements.[62]

This statement served as the DOD's official notification to Congress of the removal of the collocation restriction and the intent to implement exceptions to the Direct Combat Exclusion Rule.[63] The revised policy allowed commanders to collocate support units with women assigned (i.e., in open occupational specialties) with ground combat units. The report suggested that these changes might have the benefit of expanding career opportunities for women, while increasing flexibility for field commanders to meet combat support mission requirements, and potentially reducing the operational tempo for men assigned to collocated support units by increasing the number of personnel available for assignment.

THE REPEAL OF THE DIRECT COMBAT EXCLUSION RULE AND RECENT DEVELOPMENTS

By 2013, the military departments had opened 14,325 positions to women under the new exceptions to the exclusion rule.[64] Currently women account for 16.8% of the active duty officer corps and 15.0% of the enlisted corps across all DOD.[65] The percentage of women varies across services (see **Table 2**). The Marine Corps and Army have a lower percentage of women in the service than the Navy and Air Force, but also have a higher number of combat arms positions that have historically been closed to women. For example, in 2013 the Army reported that approximately 237,000 positions were closed to women, with over 105,000 positions in artillery, infantry and armor occupations. The Air Force, on the other hand reported less than 5,000 closed positions.[66]

Table 2. Females as a Percentage of Active Duty Personnel May 2015

	Army	Navy	Marine Corp	Air Force	Total
Female Officers	16.7%	17.2%	6.8%	20.1%	16.8%
Female Enlisted	13.4%	18.1%	7.8%	18.8%	15.0%
Total by Service	14.1%	17.9%	7.7%	19.0%	15.3%

Source: Defense Manpower Data Center.

On January 24, 2013, then-Secretary of Defense Leon Panetta announced DOD was rescinding the Direct Combat Exclusion Rule on women serving in previously restricted occupations (i.e., combat). This policy change opened two categories of positions, previously closed combat arms occupational specialties and non-combat specialties assigned to combat units (e.g., a medic serving in an infantry company). The implementation of this policy change was to be guided by the following principles:[67]

> Ensure the success of our nation's warfighting forces by preserving unit readiness, cohesion, and morale.
>
> Ensure all service men and women are given the opportunity to succeed and are set up for success with viable career paths.
>
> Retain the trust and confidence of the American people to defend this nation by promoting policies that maintain the best quality and most qualified people.
>
> Validate occupational performance standards, both physical and mental, for all military occupational specialties (MOS), specifically those that remain closed to women. Eligibility for training and development within designated occupational fields should consist of qualitative and quantifiable standards reflecting the knowledge, skills, and abilities necessary for each occupation. For occupational specialties open to women, the occupational performance standards must be gender-neutral as required by P.L. 103-160, Section 542 (sic) (1993).
>
> Ensure that a sufficient cadre of midgrade/senior women enlisted and officers are assigned to commands at the point of introduction to ensure success in the long run. This may require an adjustment to recruiting efforts, assignment processes, and personnel policies. Assimilation of

women into heretofore "closed units" will be informed by continual in-stride assessments and pilot efforts.

The Secretary of Defense directed the military departments to develop implementation plans for the review of service-level policies and standards and to expeditiously move forward in the integration of women into previously closed positions.

As per the Secretary's instruction, any recommendations to keep an occupational specialty closed to women will require approval by the Chairman of the Joint Chiefs of Staff (CJCS) and the Secretary of Defense. The opening of these positions will likely have the largest impact on the Army, Marine Corps, and the Special Operations community where infantry, armor, artillery and other specialized combat positions were previously closed to women under the Direct Combat Exclusion Rule. The military departments are expected to complete their reviews and to notify Congress of their plans for integrating women into combat roles by January 1, 2016.

Key Issues for Congress

Any changes proposed by the DOD will likely be subjected to congressional scrutiny. Congress may accept any proposed changes or seek to subject such changes to certain modifications. Two key legislative issues that may arise are the validation and implementation of gender-neutral occupational standards, and laws requiring registration for Selective Service. Among the additional issues Congress may consider are equal opportunity, unit readiness and cohesion, and force structure and manpower needs.

"Gender-Neutral" Standards

One of the issues for Congress to consider with the opening of combat roles to women is how the definition of gender-neutral standards will be applied and how the standards will be validated. The military departments, in their respective women in the service implementation plans, have indicated that they will conduct research and reviews to validate the physical standards for all occupations (opened and closed). Congress has the authority to review the proposed changes, provide oversight for implementation, and to amend the definition of gender-neutral occupational performance standards as needed.

Definitions and Requirements

In the National Defense Authorization Act for FY1994 (P.L. 103-160 §543, as amended by P.L. 113-66 §523), Congress established requirements for gender-neutral occupational performance standards:

> (1) GENDER-NEUTRAL OCCUPATIONAL STANDARD. The term "gender-neutral occupational standard", with respect to a military career designator, means that all members of the Armed Forces serving in or assigned to the military career designator must meet the same performance outcome-based standards for the successful accomplishment of the necessary and required specific tasks associated with the qualifications and duties performed while serving in or assigned to the military career designator.
>
> SEC. 543. GENDER-NEUTRAL OCCUPATIONAL PERFORMANCE STANDARDS.
>
> (a) GENDER NEUTRALITY REQUIREMENT. In the case of any military career designator that is open to both male and female members of the Armed Forces, the Secretary of Defense
>
> (1) shall ensure that qualification of members of the Armed Forces for, and continuance of members of the Armed Forces in, that occupational career field is evaluated on the basis of an occupational standard, without differential standards of evaluation on the basis of gender;
>
> (2) may not use any gender quota, goal, or ceiling except as specifically authorized by law; and
>
> (3) may not change an occupational performance standard for the purpose of increasing or decreasing the number of women in that occupational career field.
>
> (b) REQUIREMENTS RELATING TO USE OF SPECIFIC PHYSICAL REQUIREMENTS.
>
> (1) For any military career designator for which the Secretary of Defense determines that specific physical requirements for muscular strength and endurance and cardiovascular capacity are essential to the performance of duties, the Secretary shall prescribe specific physical requirements as part of the gender-neutral occupational standard for members in that career designator and shall ensure (in the case of a career designator that is open to both male and female members of the Armed Forces) that those requirements are applied on a gender-neutral basis.
>
> (2) Whenever the Secretary establishes or revises a physical requirement for a military career designator, a member serving in that military career designator when the new requirement becomes effective, who is otherwise considered to be a satisfactory performer, shall be provided a reasonable period, as determined under regulations prescribed by the Secretary, to meet the standard established by the new

requirement. During that period, the new physical requirement may not be used to disqualify the member from continued service in that military career designator.

Review and Validation

All of the military departments establish testable minimum physical fitness standards for their personnel regardless of the military occupational specialty or career designator.[68] These physical fitness tests are administered upon entry and annually thereafter and are intended to encourage a minimum standard of physical fitness and health across the military forces. The standards and scoring table vary by both age and gender to account for physiological differences. For example, a 22-year old male is required to run 2 miles in a maximum time of 17:30 in order to pass the Army Physical Fitness Test (PFT). The maximum time for a 22-year-old female is 20:36. In both instances, the individuals who achieve a passing time on the run receive the same score. The scoring tables differ under the principle that a women who is able to run 2 miles in 17:30 is, on average, more physically fit (in terms of muscular strength and endurance, and cardiovascular capacity) than a man of the same age who is able to complete the run in the same time.

While all servicemembers must maintain basic physical fitness standards, the military departments also establish additional standards for entry into certain occupational fields based on the capabilities needed to complete tasks associated with that occupation. (See sample Marine Corps infantry squad assessment tasks in the below box.) Whereas basic physical standards described above are used as a mechanism to measure the servicemember's fitness, occupational standards are used to measure the ability to meet job requirements. A basic interpretation of Section 543(1)(b) regarding physical requirements suggests there will only be a common outcome-based standard for each occupational career field and that men and women would be required to meet the same physical standards in order to be similarly assigned. It follows, for example, that if the occupation requires the servicemember to run 2 miles in 17:30 minutes, both men and women must meet that standard regardless of relative fitness levels.

Some have expressed concerns that the physical occupational standards and testing for certain career fields do not accurately reflect the actual job requirements and may be unnecessarily high, creating artificial barriers to women's entry into some career fields. In the Carl Levin and Howard P. "Buck" McKeon National Defense Authorization Act for Fiscal Year 2015 (P.L. 113-291 §524), Congress gave further direction to the Secretaries of the military departments regarding the development and validation of gender-neutral occupational standards, requiring that the standards

> (1) accurately predict performance of actual, regular, and recurring duties of a military occupation; and
> (2) are applied equitably to measure individual capabilities.[69]

The first validation criteria would require evidence that the tested standard is predictive of the actual task required to serve in that occupational field. For example, one occupational requirement might be the ability to rappel down a rope from a helicopter in a certain amount of time. For practical reasons (i.e., cost, risk of injury, resource availability) it may not be in the best interest of the services to test servicemembers in a live environment. However, the number of pull-ups a servicemember can achieve may be predictive of their performance in rappelling. Under the criteria above, the services would be required to demonstrate both that rappelling from a helicopter is a regular requirement for the occupational specialty, and that the pull-up standard is an accurate measure of a servicemember's ability to achieve that task regardless of gender.

Sample Marine Corps Infantry Squad Assessment Tasks

Day 1:

- Hike one kilometer uphill with 28-pound assault pack and personal weapon.
- Scramble over 8-foot shipping container with weapons.
- Set weapons to Condition One and conduct a live-fire movement to contact with pop-up targets at 100, 200, and 300 meters.
- Regroup and repel a "counterattack" with pop-up targets.
- Conduct "casualty evacuation" moving a 214-pound dummy 50 meters and back in teams of two or four.
- Allow engineers to move forward and fire two breaching shots with Bangalore torpedoes.

Day 2:

- Hike seven kilometers with weapons and 59-pound packs.
- Dig fighting holes for two hours in two-man teams, alternating on and off every 15 minutes.

Source: U.S. Marine Corps as reported in Seck, Hope H., "Pushing the Boundaries; All-female Marine Grunt Teams get Creative During Experiment," *Marine Corps Times,* May 11, 2015.

Note: The tasks above are part of the women in combat assessments that the Marine Corps is conducting the the Ground Combat Element Integrated Task Force (GCEITF). For each specialty there are different tasks and male and female volunteers are randomly assigned to squad positions that operate on a two-day assessment cycle with one day off.

While the focus for validating these requirements is on the military career occupations previously closed to women, the services are also evaluating whether standards should differ for other occupational specialties. Comments from General Martin Dempsey, Chairman of the Joint Chief of Staff suggested that in validating requirements, they will be taking into account these issues[70]

> as we look at the requirements for a spectrum of conflict, not just COIN, counterinsurgency, we really need to have standards that apply across all of those. Importantly, though, if we do decide that a particular standard is so high that a woman couldn't make it, the burden is now on the service to come back and explain to the secretary, why is it that high? Does it really have to be that high?

The military departments are in the process of reviewing and validating performance standards and expect to have initial results by September of 2015. In addition to other review efforts, the Marine Corps and the Army have been conducting assessments of women's performance in their elite infantry training schools. In 2012, the U.S. Marine Corps temporarily opened its Infantry Officer Course (IOC) and its enlisted Infantry Training Battalion (ITB) to female volunteers. As of May 2015, the end of the Marine Corps experiment, 29 female officers had attempted the course but none had graduated.[71] The pass rate for women in the enlisted Marine Corps Infantry Training Battalion (ITB), which is regarded as a less strenuous course than the IOC, has been 35% over the testing period compared with a 98% pass rate for males entering the course.[72]

Likewise, the Army in 2015 opened its Ranger School to women for the first time for a one-time integrated assessment of female performance in the school. Of the 113 women who tried to qualify for the school, only 20 qualified, and 19 started the course.[73] Of all those who start the course, the historical graduation rate at Ranger School is about 40%.[74] As of May 2015, 8 of the 19 women had made it through the first assessment (Ranger Assessment

Phase or "RAP week") but did not pass the Darby Phase[75] to qualify for the next step of training. Three of the eight women were invited to restart the Ranger School from day one in June 2015. On August 17, 2015, the Army announced that two women would be the first female soldiers to graduate from the Ranger School. The female graduates will be eligible to wear the Ranger tab on their uniforms signifying their achievement; however, they are not yet eligible to serve in combat occupations in the 75th Ranger Regiment.[76]

Implementation Concerns

Whether the standards are changed or stay the same as a result of the DOD's review, many have concerns about the implementation. Although there are women who can meet and exceed the existing physical standards for males, forcing women to meet higher standards has been found in some cases to increase their injury and attrition rates.[77] In the Canadian experience in which women were recruited for a 16-week infantry training course that was identical to the men's course, the outcome was described as the "high cost of recruiting women that yielded poor results."[78] Additionally, a recent study of women in close ground combat from the United Kingdom Ministry of Defense (MoD) found that in initial military training, women have twice as much risk of musculoskeletal injury as men, and 15% to 20% higher rates of non-battle injuries in recent operations.[79] However, this MoD report also acknowledged that women who would be capable of passing the close ground combat training might be more physically fit and less prone to injury than a cohort of women entering initial basic training.

Some are concerned that any change in standards would affect readiness and unit cohesion. Others argue that changing the current physical standards to account for male-female physiological differences would reduce unit effectiveness and ability to meet certain battlefield challenges. Some believe that even if the validation process shows that current standards for certain occupational series are inappropriate or unnecessarily high, any changes at this particular time would be perceived as a lowering of standards solely for the purpose of including women. For example, some are concerned that unit morale or cohesion might be affected if the integration of women under new standards creates the perception that the woman has not "earned" her place or that she is potentially replacing a more capable male soldier.[80]

Options for Congress

Women's advocacy groups and other military and veterans' groups are likely to closely monitor DOD's review process and announcement for occupational standards. By law (P.L. 103-160 §543), DOD must notify Congress of changes to occupational standards that affect women's entry into previously closed military career designators prior to implementing the standards:

> (c) NOTICE TO CONGRESS OF CHANGES- Whenever the Secretary of Defense proposes to implement changes to the gender-neutral occupational standards for a military career designator that are expected to result in an increase, or in a decrease, of at least 10 percent in the number of female members of the Armed Forces who enter, or are assigned to, that military career designator, the Secretary of Defense shall submit to Congress a report providing notice of the change and the justification and rationale for the change. Such changes may then be implemented only after the end of the 60-day period beginning on the date on which such report is submitted.[81]

Congress may then postpone implementation, request further studies, reviews or justification, or allow the changes go into effect.

Selective Service

Many of those who emphasize equal rights say it is more difficult for servicemembers to advance to top-ranking positions in the armed services without combat experience. The inability of women to serve in combat roles is thus seen as a barrier to equal opportunity for promotion and selection for leadership roles.[82] Some carry the argument further to say women cannot be equal in society as long as they are barred from full participation in all levels of the national security system.[83] In their view, modern weapons have equalized the potential for women in combat since wars are less likely to be fought on a hand-to-hand basis. In this regard, properly trained women would be able to perform successfully in combat and exempting them from serving in combat is unfair to men.

This leads some to argue that equal access to combat jobs also obliges women to take equal responsibility for registering for selective service and being subject to the draft.[84] Women are divided on this issue with some saying they should be allowed in combat but many saying they should not be forced into combat.[85] Critics contend it would be unfair to permit women a choice that is not available to men and to make the choice available to both men and women would make it difficult for the services to function, especially in the event of war or national emergency. Given this argument, Congress may consider not only whether women who *want* to serve in combat roles are allowed to, but if women should be *required* to serve in combat roles.

Options for Congress

The question of whether women should be required to register for Selective Service under current law was previously decided by the Supreme Court in the 1981 majority decision in *Rostker v. Goldberg*. In the majority opinion, Justice William Rehnquist wrote:

> [t]he existence of the combat restrictions clearly indicates the basis for Congress' decision to exempt women from registration. The purpose of registration was to prepare for a draft of combat troops. Since women are excluded from combat, Congress concluded that they would not be needed in the event of a draft, and therefore decided not to register them.[86]

Congress has a number of options in addressing this issue. Congress has the authority to change draft registration laws (that currently pertain only to males) to include women.[87] It has also been suggested that this issue can be made moot by terminating Selective Service registration. Another option for Congress might be to keep the draft registration laws unchanged, only requiring males to register. However, if Congress keeps the status quo, it is also possible *Rostker v. Goldberg* could be overturned in a future court ruling.

Other Concerns Regarding Women in Combat

Supporters of opening more occupational specialties and units to women note that women are already serving, fighting, and dying in combat. Others argue that opening more roles to women will result in a bigger pool of eligible recruits to compete for occupational assignments and could result in higher performing units. Some contend that unless all military roles are opened to women, women will not have equal career leadership opportunities.

Those opposed to changing restrictions on women in combat roles argue that a lack of combat experience does not adversely affect career advancement and promotions for women. They argue further that the progress of women is not the most important issue at hand, and contend that military readiness and national security has been and would further be weakened due to the presence of women in combat units.[88] Those opposed note that close combat situations have and continue to exist and, on average, an all-male unit would be higher-performing in those types of engagements due to physical differences.

Both those in favor and opposed to women in combat acknowledge that there are likely social, cultural, and administrative barriers that would need to be overcome in order to implement full integration of women into combat units. Some of these administrative barriers (such as barrack/berthing assignments and separate toilet/shower facilities) have been overcome in the past as women were integrated into other occupational specialties and units.

In past gender integration efforts, the services have sought to assign senior female officers and non-commissioned to units prior to the assignment of more junior enlisted and attempted to avoid assigning only one women to a unit.[89] Developing appropriate assignment policies may be more challenging as the number of women qualifying for combat roles may initially be very small as a percentage of the total force. For example, in the Marine Corps, where women account for only 7.7% of the total force, an infantry squad might consist of only one or two women out of twelve Marines, while other squads might have no women at all assigned.[90]

In terms of cultural adaptation, individuals who are accustomed to being in all-male units may offer some resistance to change. Some are also concerned that in small unit settings male-female relationships might develop that could affect unit cohesion and morale and result in reduced unit performance. Others note that women have been integrated into units for extended deployment periods with close-quarter environments for much of the recent history of the military. They also point to other factors, beyond gender homogeneity, that contribute to positive unit cohesion such as shared experiences, leadership, and command climate. Some also note that some of the same arguments about social cohesion were historically used by those opposed to the integration of other minority groups in the military (e.g., racial minorities and homosexuals) and that there is little or no evidence that unit effectiveness was reduced as a result of that integration.

Outlook for Congress

The military departments, as part of their women in combat implementation plans, are studying some of these social cohesion and morale concerns to understand the possible impact of change and to develop potential mitigation strategies. All DOD reviews and studies are expected to be completed by September 2015. The military departments are expected to present their results and findings to the Secretary of Defense for approval authority and the Secretary is required to notify Congress of DOD's plans for integrating women into combat roles no later than January 1, 2016.

APPENDIX. KEY LEGISLATIVE AND POLICY ACTIONS

Table A-1. Timeline of Key Legislative and Policy Actions for Integration of Women in the Armed Services 1901-2014

Year	Key Legislative and Policy Actions	Law
1901	Army Nurse Corps is established under the Army Reorganization Act of 1901.	31 Stat. 753; February 2, 1901
1908	Navy Nurse Corps is established.	P.L. 115; 35 Stat. 146; May 13, 1908
1942	Naval Reserve is opened to Women and the Women's Army Auxiliary Corps is created.	P.L. 689; 56 Stat. 730; July 30, 1942; P.L. 554, 56 Stat. 278, May 14, 1942
1943	Marine Corps Women's Reserve is established and the Women's Army Corps is established as part of the regular Army on a temporary basis.	P.L. 110; 57 Stat. 371; July 1, 1943
1948	Women's Armed Services Integration Act of 1948 makes women a permanent part of the military, but prohibits their assignment to combatant aircraft and naval vessels and limits the proportion of women in the military to 2% of enlisted and 10% of officers.	P.L. 625; 62 Stat. 356; June 12, 1948
1967	Limits on the percent of women in the military are repealed.	P.L. 90-130; 81 Stat. 374; November 8, 1967

Year	Key Legislative and Policy Actions	Law
1974	Minimum age requirement for women enlisting without parental consent is reduced from 18 to 17 to be consistent with age of consent for men.	P.L. 93-290; 88 Stat. 173; May 24, 1974
1975	Women are allowed to be admitted to service academies.	P.L. 94-106; 89 Stat. 537; October 7, 1975
1978	Women are permitted to be assigned permanent duty on noncombatant Navy ships and up to six months of temporary duty on other ships.	P.L. 95-485; 92 Stat. 1623;October 20, 1978
1988	DOD implements "risk rule" which excludes women form noncombat units or missions if the risk of exposure to direct combat, hostile fire, or capture were equal to or greater than the risks in the combat units they support.	NA
1991	The Presidential Commission on the Assignment of Women in the Armed Forces is established.	P.L. 102-190; 105 Stat. 1365; December 5, 1991
1993	Congress establishes requirements for gender-neutral occupational standards and repeals prohibition of women serving on combatant aircraft and vessels.	P.L. 103-160; 107 Stat. 1659 et seq.; November 30, 1993
1994	The "risk rule" is rescinded and DOD issues the Direct Ground Combat and Assignment Rule which limits women frombeing assigned to units below brigade level whose primary mission is to engage in direct combat on the ground.	NA
2000	Congress mandates 30-day (in-session) notice of any change that would open assignment of women to Navy submarines.	P.L. 106-398; 114 Stat. 1654A-136; October 30, 2000
2006	Congress mandates 30-day (in-session) notification for any change to the 1994 ground combat exclusion policy, or the opening or closing of military career fields to women.	P.L. 109-163; 119 Stat. 3251; January 6, 2006

Table A-1. (Continued)

Year	Key Legislative and Policy Actions	Law
2008	The Military Leadership Diversity Commission is established with mandate to reviewpromotion and command opportunities in the Armed Services by ethnicity and gender.	P.L. 110-417; 122 Stat. 4476; October 14, 2008
2010	DOD notifies Congress of intent to allow women to serve on submarines.	NA
2011	Congress mandates review of the Direct Ground Combat and Assignment Rule.	P.L. 111-383; 214 Stat.4217; January 7, 2011
2012	DOD eliminates the colocation restriction from the Direct Ground Combat and Assignment Rule.	NA
2013	DOD repeals the Direct Ground Combat and Assignment Rule, removing barriers to the assignment of women to combat units and occupations and directs implementation by January 1, 2016.	NA
2014	Congress issues validation criteria for the development of gender-neutral occupational standards.	P.L. 113-291; 128 Stat.1919; September 19, 2014

Source: Compiled by CRS from multiple sources.

End Notes

1 Defense Manpower Data Center, Defense Casualty Analysis System. GWOT includes Operation Enduring Freedom, Operation Iraqi Freedom, and Operation New Dawn.

2 Bensahel, Nora, David Barno, and Katherine Kidder, et al., *Battlefields and Boardrooms; Women's Leadership in the Military and the Private Sector*, Center for New American Security, January 2015, p. 9. The Silver Star Medal is the third-highest military decoration for valor to be awarded to members of the uniformed services.

3 Department of Defense, *Defense Department Rescinds Direct Combat Exclusion Rule; Services to Expand Integration of Women into Previously Restricted Occupations and Units*, Press Release, January 24, 2013.

4 The military departments were required to submit "Women in the Services Review (WISR) Implementation Plans" to the Secretary of Defense to outline their plans for opening closed occupations and positions to women by the 2016 deadline. The WISR implementation plans for the Army, Navy, Marine Corps, Air Force and U.S. Special Operations Command

(USSOCOM) can be found at http://www.defense.gov/releases/release.aspx?releaseid=16102.

[5] Congress has the authority "To make Rules for the Government and Regulation of the land and naval Forces." U.S. Constitution, Article 1, Section 8, clause 14.

[6] James, Edward T., Janet Wilson James, and Paul S. Boyer, et al., *Notable American Women 1607-1950: A Biographical Dictionary*, vol. 2, pp. 385-386.

[7] 31 Stat. 753; February 2, 1901.

[8] P.L. 115; 35 Stat. 146; May 13, 1908.

[9] P.L. 689; 56 Stat. 730; July 30, 1942.

[10] P.L. 554, 56 Stat. 278, May 14, 1942.

[11] "That there is hereby established in the Army of the United States, for the period of the present war and for six months thereafter or for such shorter period as the Congress by concurrent resolution or the President by proclamation shall prescribe, a component to be known as the 'Women's Army Corps'." P.L. 110; 57 Stat. 371; July 1, 1943.

[12] Women in the Military Service for America Memorial Foundation, Inc., see http://www.womensmemorial.org/H&C/ History/wwii.html.

[13] Ibid.; Sixty-seven Army nurses and 11 Navy nurses were captured in the Philippines and held by the Japanese for nearly 3 years. Five Navy nurses were captured on the island of Guam were held as POWs for four months. One Army flight nurse was aboard an aircraft that was shot down behind enemy lines in Germany in 1944 and was held as a POW for four months.

[14] P.L. 625; 62 Stat. 356; June 12, 1948: "Women's Armed Services Integration Act of 1948."

[15] This legislation did not bar women from ground combat roles.

[16] Janowitz, Morris, and Charles C. Moskos, Five Years of the All-Volunteer Force: 1973-1978, *Armed Forces and Society*, V, February 1979: 171-218.

[17] P.L. 90-130; 81 Stat. 374; November 8, 1967.

[18] P.L. 93-290; 88 Stat. 173; May 24, 1974. Prior to enacting this law, males who were not less than 17 years of age could enlist, while females were required to be at least 18 years of age.

[19] P.L. 94-106; 89 Stat. 537; October 7, 1975. Women had already been admitted to the Coast Guard and Merchant Marine Academies by administrative action. Women had also participated in the Air Force Reserve Officer Training Course (ROTC) as a source of commissioning between 1954 through 1958, but it was not until 1969 that women were again allowed into the Air Force Program, and in 1972 the Army and Navy opened ROTC as a commissioning source for women.

[20] P.L. 95-97; 91 Stat. 327; July 30, 1977.

[21] P.L. 95-485; 92 Stat. 1623; October 20, 1978.

[22] U.S. Congress, Senate, Committee on Armed Services, Requiring Reinstitution of Registration for Certain Persons under the Military Selective Service Act, and For Other Reasons, Rept. 96-226, 96th Cong., 1st Sess., June 19, 1979.

[23] U.S. Army Women's Museum, available at http://www.history.army.mil/html/museums/showcase/women/awm_text.html.

[24] Raines, Edgar F., Jr., The Rucksack War: U.S. Army Operational Logistics in Grenada, 1983, Center of Military History: Washington, DC, 2010: 494.

[25] Department of Defense, *Report of the Task Force on Women in the Military*, January 1988, p.10.

[26] Combat jobs include those that directly confront and engage the enemy, such as infantry; combat-related jobs include those that support combat units in the field, such as those in support positions with combat engineers, as well as infantry and tank support units, including units that transport fuel, ordinance and ammunition.

[27] The remaining positions were closed due to prohibitive living arrangements (12%) and special operations assignments (2%). The GAO's study did not look at how this affected women's advancement or promotion opportunities. U.S. General Accounting Office, *Information on DOD's Assignment Policy and Direct Ground Combat Definition*, GAO/NSIAD-99-7, October 1988: 4. See also U.S. General Accounting Office, *Women in the Military Impact of Proposed Legislation to Open More Combat Support Position and Units to Women*, GAO/NSIAD-88- 197BR, July 1988.

[28] Women in the Military Service for America Memorial Foundation, Inc., see http://www.womensmemorial.org/H&C/ History/wwii.html.

[29] Sciolino, Elaine, "Female P.O.W. Is Abused, Kindling Debate," *New York Times*, June 29, 1992.

[30] P.L. 102-190; 105 Stat. 1365; December 5, 1991.

[31] Presidential Commission on the Assignment of Women in the Armed Forces, Report to the President, November 15, 1992.

[32] For more information on special operations forces, please see CRS Report RS21048, *U.S. Special Operations Forces (SOF): Background and Issues for Congress*, by Andrew Feickert.

[33] P.L. 103-160; 107 Stat. 1659 et seq.; November 30, 1993.

[34] A brigade or its equivalent is a unit of approximately 3,000-5,000 persons.

[35] Department of Defense, *Direct Ground Combat Definition and Assignment Rule*, January 13, 1994.

[36] Department of Defense, *Direct Ground Combat Definition and Assignment Rule*, January 13, 1994.

[37] Specialist Lori Piestewa became the first woman to be killed in the 2003 invasion of Iraq from injuries sustained in the attack. However, much of the attention focused on PFC Jessica Lynch after various conflicting accounts of her actions were published and reports suggested that certain injuries she sustained were the result of sexual assault while in captivity. Some pointed to this as an argument against women in combat roles. See U.S. Congress, House Committee on Oversight and Government Reform, *Misleading Information From the Battlefield: The Tillman and Lynch Episodes*, First Report, 110th Cong., 2nd sess., September 16, 2008, H.Rept. 110-858 (Washington: GPO, 2008).

[38] For more information see CRS Report RL32476, *U.S. Army's Modular Redesign: Issues for Congress*, by Andrew Feickert.

[39] Perry, Tony, "Women on Iraq's Front Lines," *Los Angeles Times*, November 13, 2008.

[40] Wood, Sara, "Woman Soldier Receives Silver Star for Valor in Iraq," *DOD News*, June 16, 2005.

[41] Cronk, Terry M., "Cultural Support Team Women Serve with Distinction," *DOD News*, April 30, 2015.

[42] Fainaru, Steve, "Silver Stars Affirm One Unit's Mettle," *Washington Post*, June 26, 2005.

[43] P.L. 109-163; 119 Stat. 3251; January 6, 2006. As described in this law, "such a change may then be implemented only after the end of a period of 30 days of continuous session of Congress (excluding any day on which either House of Congress is not in session) following the date on which the report is received."

[44] The Army policy defines direct combat to include the closing with the enemy in order to "destroy or capture the enemy, *or while repelling the enemy's assault by fire, close combat, or counterattack*." [Emphasis added.] Headquarter, U.S. Department of the Army, 1992, p. 5.

[45] Harrell, Margaret C., et al., Assessing the Assignment Policy for Army Women, RAND, National Defense Research Institute, 2007: xvii.

[46] The Combat Action Badge recognizes soldiers who have engaged the enemy, or were engaged by the enemy during combat operation. See http://www.army.mil/symbols/CombatBadges/action.html.

[47] Harrell, Margaret C., et al., Assessing the Assignment Policy for Army Women, RAND, National Defense Research Institute, 2007: xxi.

[48] Lorber, Janie, "Quiet Resistance to Women on Subs," *New York Times*, May 12, 2010.

[49] "Pentagon Panel Says Women Should Serve on Subs," *CNN U.S.*, May 26, 2000.

[50] "Lawmaker moves to bar women from subs," *Washington Times*, May 5, 2000.

[51] P.L. 106-398; 114 Stat. 1654 A-136; October 30, 2000.

[52] "Pentagon OKs Lifting the Ban on Women in Submarines," *Reuters*, February 23, 2010.

[53] Faram, Mark D., "First Enlisted Female Sub Selectees Announced," *Navy Times*, June 22, 2015.

[54] P.L. 110-417; 122 Stat. 4476; October 14, 2008; see §596.

[55] Lieutenant Colonel for Army, Marine Corps and Air Force, and Commander for Navy and Coast Guard.

[56] Military Leadership Diversity Commission, 1851 South Bell Street, Arlington, VA, 22202. Although the Final Report was issued on-line on March 7, 2011, the routing letter from the Chairman to the President and Congress was dated March 15, 2011.

[57] Military Leadership Diversity Commission, *Final Report*, pp. 127, 129 and 130.

[58] Daniel, Lisa, "Panel says Rescind Policy on Women in Combat," *American Forces Press Service*, March 8, 2011.

[59] P.L. 111-383; 214 Stat. 4217; January 7, 2011.

[60] "At present, DOD's Direct Combat assignment Rule (DGCAR) policy states that women can be assigned to all positions for which they are qualified, except within units below the brigade level whose primary mission is to engage in direct combat on the ground. The Army collocation assignment restriction further states that women can serve in any officer or enlisted specialty or position, except in those specialties, positions or units (battalion size or smaller) which are assigned a routine mission to engage in direct combat, or which collocated routinely with units assigned a direct combat mission." http://www.armyg1.army.mil/hr/witai

[61] Department of Defense, Office of the Under Secretary of Defense (P&R), *Report to Congress on the Reviews of Laws, Policies and Regulations Restricting the Service of Female Members in the U.S. Armed Forces*, February, 2012, p. 4.

[62] Department of Defense, *Report to Congress on the Reviews of Laws, Policies and Regulations Restricting the Service of Female Members in the U.S. Armed Forces*, February 2012, p. 4.

[63] The report also stated that DOD gave notice of the changes commencing the congressional review timeline required in 10 U.S.C.§652, which means these changes became policy since Congress did not act on them.

[64] Department of Defense, *Memo from the Chairmen of the Joint Chiefs of Staff to the Secretary of Defense on Women in the Service Implementation Plan*, January 9, 2013.

[65] Defense Manpower Data Center as of January 2015.

[66] Roulo, Claudette, "Defense Department Expands Women's Combat Role," *DOD News*, January 2013.

[67] Department of Defense, *Memo from the Chairmen of the Joint Chiefs of Staff to the Secretary of Defense on Women in the Service Implementation Plan*, January 9, 2013.

[68] Some occupational specialties require servicemembers to meet additional physical standards.

[69] P.L. 113-291; 128 Stat. 1919; September 19, 2014.

[70] Winn, Pete, "Gen. Dempsey: If Women Can't Meet Military Standard, Pentagon Will Ask 'Does it Really Have to Be That High," *cnsnews.com*, January 25, 2013.

[71] Seck, Hope H., "Last IOC in Marine Infantry Experiment Drops Female Officers," *Marine Corps Times,* April 8, 2015.

[72] Data provided to CRS by the U.S. Marine Corps in March 2015.

[73] Mulrine, Anna, "Breaking Military's Ultimate Glass Ceiling? Women start Ranger Training.," *The Christian Science Monitor*, April 30, 2015.

[74] Lamothe, Dan, "Will the Army Open its Elite Ranger Regiment to Women? A Controversial Decision Awaits," *Washington Post*, August 11, 2015.

[75] The Darby Phase is 15 days of intensive squad training and operations in a field environment that includes an advanced obstacle course, airborne training, and a series of student-let and cadre-led patrols.

[76] The 75th Ranger Regiment is a light infantry special operations unit specializing in a range of missions including direct action and personnel recovery. The Army has not yet announced whether it will allow women to apply for positions in this regiment or whether it will request a waiver to keep these positions closed.

[77] Scarborough, Rowan, "Army may Train Women for Rigor of Front Lines, Studies Predict Injury, Attrition," *Washington Times*, July 30, 2012.

[78] Moore, Molly, Canada Puts Women on Front Line, *Los Angeles Times*, November 23, 1989.

[79] United Kingdom Ministry of Defense, *Women in ground close combat (GCC) review paper*, December 1, 2014, p. B1, https://www.gov.uk/government/publications/women-in-ground-close-combat-gcc-review-paper.

[80] In studies of mixed gender units, some servicemembers attributed unit cohesion issues to differential standards between men and women. See for example Harrell, Margaret C. and Laura L. Miller, *New Opportunities for Military Women; Effects Upon Readiness, Cohesion, and Morale*, Santa Monica, CA, January 1997, p. 78.

[81] Given that there are currently zero women in some career designators, an increase of one woman would be an increase of over 10%.

[82] Bacon, Lance M., "We Need Their Talent," *Army Times*, October 24, 2011. Odierno: "This is about managing talent. We have incredibly talented females who should be in those positions. We have work to do within the [Department of Defense] to get them to recognize and change."

[83] In July 2015 a teenage girl from New Jersey brought a federal class action suit against the Selective Service claiming the refusal to allow women to register is discriminatory now that women are eligible for combat roles.

[84] Mulrine, Anna, "With U.S. Women Soon Eligible for Combat, the Draft Could be Next," *The Christian Science Monitor*, October 28, 2014.

[85] Lafond, Nicole, "Poll: Most Women Believe They Should Not Be Forced Into Combat," *The Daily Caller*, February 7, 2013.

[86] *Rostker v. Goldberg*, 453 U.S. 57 (1981).

[87] 50 U.S.C.§453.

[88] See for example Center for Military Readiness, "Problematic Proposals in National Defense Authorization Act for 2015 (NDAA)," at http://www.cmrlink.org/content/women-in-combat/37616/ problematic_proposals_in_national_defense_authorization_act_for_2015_ndaa.

[89] See for example the Navy's policy on assignment of women to surface vessels (OPNAVINST 1300.17B, May 27, 2001) which requires a minimum of two female officers to be assigned

(when no female enlisted are assigned) and a minimum of one female officer and one female Chief Petty Officer to be assigned to all gender integrated ships.

[90] Seck, Hope Hodge, "All-Female Marine Grunt Team Gets Innovative During Combat Tests," *Marine Corps Times*, May 2015.

In: Combat Service Opportunities for Women ISBN: 978-1-63484-432-1
Editor: Cassandra Schultz

Chapter 2

MILITARY PERSONNEL: DOD IS EXPANDING COMBAT SERVICE OPPORTUNITIES FOR WOMEN, BUT SHOULD MONITOR LONG-TERM INTEGRATION PROGRESS*

United States Government Accountability Office

WHY GAO DID THIS STUDY

Since September 2001 more than 300,000 women have been deployed in Iraq and Afghanistan, where more than 800 women have been wounded and more than 130 have died. A 1994 rule prohibited women from being assigned to many direct ground- combat units, but on January 24, 2013, the Secretary of Defense and the Chairman of the Joint Chiefs of Staff rescinded the rule and directed the military services to open closed positions and occupations to women by January 1, 2016.

Senate Report 113-176 had a provision for GAO to review the services' progress in opening closed positions and occupations to women. This report assesses the (1) status of service efforts to open positions and occupations to women, including steps to identify and mitigate potential challenges; (2) extent the services' efforts to validate gender-neutral occupational standards are consistent with statutory and Joint Staff requirements; and (3) extent DOD

* This is an edited, reformatted and augmented version of the United States Government Accountability Office publication, GAO-15-589, dated July 2015.

is tracking, monitoring, and providing oversight of the services' integration plans. GAO analyzed statutes, DOD guidance, and service reports and plans, and interviewed DOD officials.

WHAT GAO RECOMMENDS

GAO recommends that DOD develop plans to monitor integration progress after January 2016. DOD concurred with GAO's recommendation. GAO previously recommended that DOD establish a process of periodically reevaluating DOD's requirements for the Selective Service System. DOD has not taken action but GAO continues to believe the recommendation is valid.

WHAT GAO FOUND

The military services and U.S. Special Operations Command (SOCOM) have opened selected positions and occupations to women since January 2013, as shown in the table below, and are determining whether to open the remaining closed positions and occupations. The services and SOCOM also are conducting studies to identify and mitigate potential integration challenges in areas such as unit cohesion, women's health, and facilities. As of May 2015, the Secretary of the Navy was the only military department Secretary to recommend an exception to policy to keep positions closed to women on three classes of ships that are scheduled to be decommissioned, due in part to high retrofit costs.

The services and SOCOM are working to address statutory and Joint Staff requirements for validating gender-neutral occupational standards. GAO identified five elements required for standards validation. GAO compared these elements to the services' and SOCOM's planned methodologies and determined that their study plans contained steps that, if carried out as planned, potentially address all five elements. However, the services' and SOCOM's efforts are still underway; therefore, GAO could not assess the extent that the studies will follow the planned methodologies or report how the study results will be implemented.

Table: Changes in and Status of Military Service Opportunities for Women as of March 2015

	Positions opened since January 2013	Positions closed as of March 2015	Percent of positions closed as of March 2015
Army	68,500	176,800	18%
Air Force	0	4,300	1%
Navy	17,100	9,200	2%
Marine Corps	6,000	54,800	25%
Total	**91,600**	**245,100**	—
SOCOM	7,000	25,700	41%

Source: GAO analysis of DOD data. | GAO-15-589

The Department of Defense (DOD) has been tracking, monitoring, and providing oversight of the services' and SOCOM's integration efforts, but does not have plans to monitor the services' implementation progress after January 2016 in integrating women into newly opened positions and occupations. While DOD requires the services and SOCOM to submit quarterly progress reports, this requirement ends in January 2016. Without ongoing monitoring of integration progress, it will be difficult for DOD to help the services overcome potential obstacles. Further, when opening positions to women, DOD must analyze the implications for how it meets certain resource needs. In 2012, GAO assessed the military necessity of the Selective Service System and examined alternatives to its structure. GAO recommended in 2012 that DOD establish a process of periodically reevaluating its requirements in light of changing threats, operating environments, and strategic guidance. DOD has not taken action to do this, but agreed that a thorough assessment of the issue was merited, and should include a review of the statutes and policies surrounding the registration process and the potential to include the registration of women. GAO continues to believe that DOD should establish a process of periodically reevaluating DOD's requirements for the Selective Service System.

ABBREVIATIONS

DOD	Department of Defense
OUSD(P&R)	Office of the Under Secretary of Defense for Personnel and Readiness
SOCOM	U.S. Special Operations Command

* * *

July 20, 2015

The Honorable John McCain
Chairman
The Honorable Jack Reed
Ranking Member
Committee on Armed Services
United States Senate

The Honorable Mac Thornberry
Chairman
The Honorable Adam Smith
Ranking Member
Committee on Armed Services
House of Representatives

Since September 2001, approximately 300,000 women have been deployed for contingency operations in Iraq and Afghanistan, where more than 800 women have been wounded and more than 130 have died. A 1994 rule[1] prevented women from serving in direct ground-combat positions, but on January 24, 2013, the Secretary of Defense and the Chairman of the Joint Chiefs of Staff rescinded the 1994 rule, and directed the military services to meet milestones for the full integration of women into these positions by January 1, 2016.[2] After the Department of Defense (DOD) issued the 1994 rule, we reported on various issues related to gender integration; see the list of related GAO products at the end of this report.

Senate Report No. 113-176,[3] which accompanied a proposed Senate bill for the National Defense Authorization Act for Fiscal Year 2015, included a provision for GAO to review the military services' progress in opening closed positions and occupations to women, and in developing and validating gender-neutral occupational standards. We assessed (1) the status of the services' efforts to open previously closed positions and occupations to women, including any steps to identify and mitigate potential challenges; (2) the extent to which the services' efforts to validate gender-neutral occupational standards are consistent with statutory requirements and Joint Staff guidance; and (3) the extent to which DOD is tracking, monitoring, and providing oversight over the military services' plans to complete the integration of women into direct combat positions by January 2016.

For the first objective, we reviewed military service[4] and U.S. Special Operations Command[5] (SOCOM) quarterly progress reports and congressional notifications, and interviewed officials to identify the positions and occupations that have been opened to women since January 2013, and timeframes for making recommendations about opening other positions and occupations to women, and to determine if any of the services plan to request an exception to policy to keep any positions or occupations closed to women. In addition, we requested and obtained data from the services and SOCOM on the total number of positions and occupations closed to women as of March 2015. To determine the reliability of the data provided by DOD, we obtained information on how the data were collected, managed, and used through interviews with and questionnaires to relevant officials and determined that the data presented in our findings were sufficiently reliable for the purposes of this report. We also obtained and analyzed documentation and discussed with officials any potential challenges they have identified and whether they took steps or designed possible approaches to mitigating those challenges. For our second objective, we analyzed documentation describing the services' planned scope and methodology for their ongoing efforts to validate gender-neutral occupational standards and compared it to the requirements in the governing statutes[6] and the Joint Staff guidance for validating physically demanding occupational standards.[7] We also discussed these efforts with relevant officials. For our third objective, we obtained and analyzed documentation and discussed with officials from the Office of the Under Secretary of Defense for Personnel and Readiness (OUSD(P&R)) and the Joint Staff the nature and level of their tracking and monitoring, and their review of the military services' and SOCOM's efforts to integrate women into combat positions. We then compared these efforts to DOD guidance,[8] internal control standards, and statutory requirements. Appendix I provides a more detailed discussion of our scope and methodology.

We conducted this performance audit from September 2014 to July 2015 in accordance with generally accepted government auditing standards. Those standards require that we plan and perform the audit to obtain sufficient, appropriate evidence to provide a reasonable basis for our findings and conclusions based on our audit objectives. We believe that the evidence obtained provides a reasonable basis for our findings and conclusions based on our audit objectives.

BACKGROUND

The role of women in the military has evolved from the Women's Armed Services Integration Act of 1948[9]— which afforded women the opportunity to serve in the military services—to January 2013, when the Secretary of Defense and the Chairman of the Joint Chiefs of Staff directed the services to open closed units and positions to women by January 1, 2016. Figure 1 provides details about changes in military service opportunities for women.

In January 1994, the Secretary of Defense issued the Direct Ground Combat Definition and Assignment Rule,[10] which allowed women to be assigned to almost all positions, but excluded women from assignment to units below the brigade level whose primary mission was to engage in direct ground combat.[11] The memorandum establishing the 1994 rule also permitted restrictions on assignment of women in four other instances where: (1) the service secretary attests that the costs of appropriate berthing and privacy arrangements are prohibitive; (2) the units and positions are doctrinally required to physically collocate and remain with direct ground-combat units that are closed to women; (3) the units are engaged in long-range reconnaissance operations and special operations forces missions; and (4) job-related physical requirements would necessarily exclude the vast majority of women service members. The memorandum also permitted the services to propose further restrictions on the assignment of women, together with justification for those proposed restrictions.

In 2012, DOD issued a report to Congress reviewing the laws, policies, and regulations restricting the service of female members in the armed forces.[12] In this report, the Secretary of Defense and the Chairman of the Joint Chiefs of Staff rescinded the co-location assignment restriction that had allowed the military services to prohibit the assignment of women to units and positions physically collocated with direct ground-combat units.[13] The report also contained notifications to Congress of the department's intent to open positions and occupations that had been closed under this restriction. Specifically, the Army opened 6 enlisted occupations (9,925 positions) and

3,214 positions in 80 units that had been closed to women based on the co-location restriction. Additionally, the Army, Marine Corps, and Navy requested exceptions to policy and DOD notified Congress of its intent to open positions and occupations at the battalion level within active-duty direct combat units to inform future recommendations on other positions with the potential to be opened in the future. In its report, DOD explained that the experience gained by assigning women to these positions would help the department assess the suitability and relevance of the direct ground-combat prohibition and inform future policy decisions.

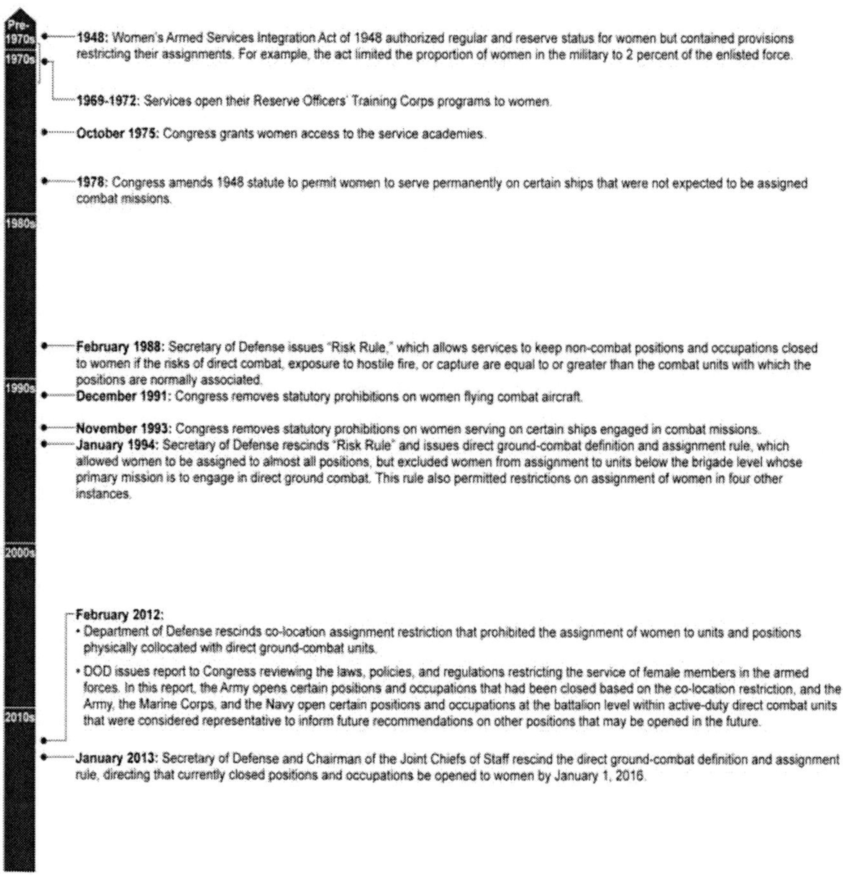

Source: GAO analysis. | GAO-15-589

Figure 1. Timeline of Changes in Military Service Opportunities for Women.

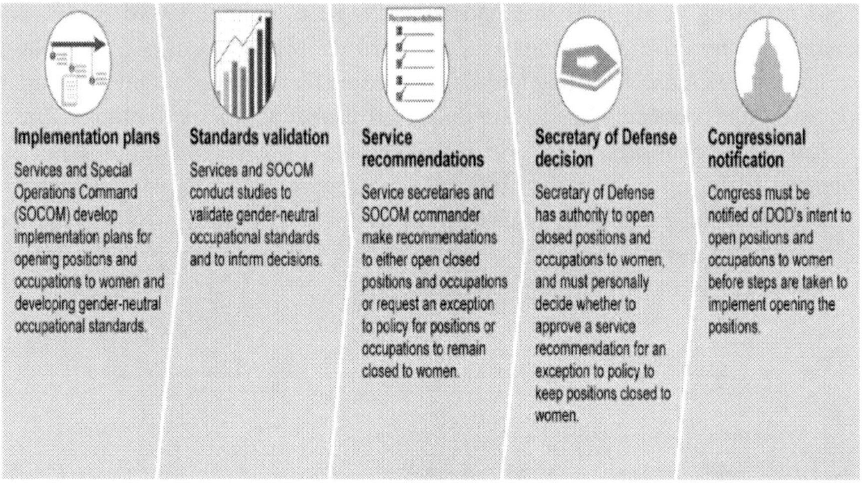

Source: GAO analysis of Department of Defence (DOD) information. | GAO-15-589

Figure 2. Overview of the Department of Defense (DOD) Process to Open Positions and Occupations to Women.

In July 2013, DOD issued a subsequent report to Congress that discussed the department's implementation of these February 2012 policy changes, the services' progress regarding elimination of gender-restrictive policy, and the rescission of the ground-combat assignment rule.[14] This report also included the total number of positions open and closed to women in each of the military services. At the time, the Navy and the Air Force had the most positions open to women (91 and 99 percent, respectively), while the Army and the Marine Corps had fewer open positions (68 and 69 percent, respectively). SOCOM also stated that in July 2013, around 46 percent of its positions were open to women.

Figure 2 generally illustrates the process used to implement the Secretary's direction to open positions and occupations that have been closed to women.

The military services traditionally have established two types of physical performance requirements. First, the military services have established general physical fitness standards to promote overall health and physical fitness among military personnel. These fitness standards apply to active and reserve servicemembers regardless of occupation and are not required by statute to be gender neutral. These standards are not intended to ensure performance in a particular occupation. Second, the services set job-specific physical performance standards to ensure that servicemembers are capable of performing the particular jobs to which they have been assigned. These job-specific standards refer to occupation-specific criteria that applicants must meet to enter or remain in a particular career field or specialty, and by statute these occupational performance standards must be gender neutral.[15]

SERVICES HAVE OPENED SELECTED POSITIONS AND OCCUPATIONS TO WOMEN, ARE DETERMINING WHETHER TO INTEGRATE DIRECT GROUND-COMBAT OCCUPATIONS, AND ARE TAKING STEPS TO IDENTIFY AND MITIGATE POTENTIAL CHALLENGES

The military services and SOCOM have opened selected positions and occupations to women since January 2013, and are in the process of determining whether to open the remaining direct ground-combat positions and occupations. As an alternative to opening a position or occupation, the Secretary of Defense permitted the services to recommend an exception to policy to keep positions or occupations closed to women; to date, the Navy is the only service to have recommended an exception to policy. The services are also conducting studies to identify integration challenges and ways to mitigate these challenges in areas such as unit cohesion, women's health, equipment, facilities (e.g., separate restrooms and sleeping quarters), women's interest in serving in ground-combat positions, and international issues. We also examined the issue of sexual assault and harassment in the integration process.

Most Services and SOCOM Have Opened Selected Positions and Occupations to Women

In response to the January 2013 memorandum, most of the services—except for the Air Force[16]—and SOCOM have opened selected positions and occupations, and the openings to date largely involve closed positions in open occupations.[17] The memorandum directed the military departments to submit detailed plans by May 15, 2013, to implement this direction to open closed positions to women, and required the implementation plans to be consistent with a set of guiding principles, goals, and milestones for the integration process. The memorandum also required the military departments to submit quarterly progress reports on implementation.[18] All four services and SOCOM developed implementation plans, including goals and milestones, which were subsequently reviewed by the Secretary of Defense in May 2013. The services and SOCOM also provided quarterly progress reports on their efforts to open closed positions and occupations to women, starting with the third quarter of fiscal year 2013. In July 2014, OUSD(P&R) granted a request by the Joint Chiefs to change the progress report cycle from quarterly to biannual. However, an OUSD(P&R) official stated that the Chairman of the Joint Chiefs of Staff continued to receive quarterly updates, and the Under Secretary of Defense for Personnel and Readiness continued to provide the Secretary of Defense with verbal quarterly updates.

As of March 2015, the services have opened positions and occupations to women as shown in table 1.

Table 1. Positions and Occupations Opened to Women by Military Service, January 2013 through March 2015

	Percent of positions open as of April 30, 2013[a]	**Positions opened since January 2013**	**Occupations opened since January 2013**
Army	73%	68,500	1[b]
Air Force	99%	0	0[c]
Navy	92%	17,100	9[d]
Marine Corps	67%	6,000	12[e]
Total	—	**91,600**	**22**
SOCOM[f]	46%[g]	7,000	0

Source: GAO analysis of Department of Defense (DOD) congressional notifications. | GAO-15-589.

Note: Table includes rounded active and reserve component position data. The number of positions opened includes previously closed positions in open occupations and positions in newly opened occupations.

[a] Data on percentage of positions opened as of April 30, 2013, are what DOD reported to Congress in July 2013. See DOD, *Report to Congress on Women in the Services Review* (July 2013).

[b] The Army has opened its combat engineer occupation since January 2013.

[c] More than 99 percent of the Air Force's occupations were open as of January 2013; its remaining closed occupations are in its battlefield airmen group, whose members are employed alone or as part of a special operations unit, joint, interagency, or coalition force.

[d] Examples of Navy occupations opened since January 2013 include sonar technicians and machinist mate auxiliary.

[e] Examples of Marine Corps occupations opened since January 2013 include ground intelligence officer and targeting acquisition officer.

[f] Service positions and occupations that are affiliated with SOCOM are included in the totals listed above for each service; they are also broken out here to show the proportion of opened positions and occupations that are special operations. All SOCOM-affiliated positions that have been opened during this period were Army positions.

[g] This percentage is as reported by SOCOM to GAO as of July 2013.

The services are working on integration plans for these positions and occupations that have been opened to women. For example, the Army is actively recruiting women to fill recently opened positions across the force, in order to place the best qualified soldiers, regardless of gender, in positions. Further, the Navy is expanding assignment opportunities for enlisted women to specific submarine classes and is participating in surveys and questionnaires to assess integration success and gather lessons learned.

Services and SOCOM Are Determining Whether to Open Remaining Closed Positions and Occupations

At the time of this report, the services and SOCOM were in the process of determining whether to open the remaining closed positions and occupations, and the timeframe for many of these recommendations was postponed until September 2015. As of March 2015, the positions and occupations that remain closed to women are shown in table 2.

As of April 2015, all of the military services and SOCOM were working on efforts, such as the standards validation studies discussed below, to inform their recommendations on whether to open the remaining closed positions and occupations to women. The services' implementation plans included timelines for making recommendations on whether to open positions and occupations to women or to request exceptions to keep positions or occupations closed. Initially, these timelines were established independently by each service and different services were scheduled to make recommendations about similar occupations at different times. For example, the Army was scheduled to make its recommendation about armor occupations in July 2015, while the Marine Corps was scheduled to make its recommendations about armor occupations in late 2014 and early 2015. Subsequently, service officials have stated that some of those recommendation timeframes have shifted to a later point to synchronize with the Marine Corps recommendations that are now scheduled to occur in late September and early October 2015, as shown in figure 3. One reason provided by Air Force officials to support the timeline shifts was to consider impacts of another services' recommendation to open a closed occupation or position, such as when there is no viable career path in an occupation because the majority of positions serve with another services' closed unit. Another reason expressed by Army officials was that the service heads recognize the need for coordination when making recommendations about similar occupations such as infantry. An OUSD(P&R) official explained that there has always been a desire to align the recommendation timelines, and that when service timelines started to shift in 2014, the topic was extensively discussed in various meetings.

Table 2. Positions and Occupations That Remain Closed to Women by Military Service as of March 2015

	Closed positions In open occupations	**Closed positions in closed occupations**	**Total positions**	**Percent of positions closed**	**Closed occupations**	**Total occupations**	**Percent ofoverall occupations closed**
Army	1,700[a]	175,100	1,000,000	18%	21[b]	465	5%
Air Force	25	4,300	464,900	1%	6[c]	374	2%
Navy	5,300	3,900	381,600	2%	5[d]	171	3%
Marine Corps	16,700	38,100	223,300	25%	21[e]	336	6%
Total	**23,725**	**221,400**	-	-	**53**	-	-
SOCOM[f]	7,100	18,600	63,200	41%	17[g]	17	100%[h]

Source: GAO analysis of military service data. | GAO-15-589

Note: Table includes rounded active and reserve component position data for closed primary occupations. A closed position in an open occupation means that while the occupation is open to women, specific positions within certain units are closed to women (e.g., administration clerk in a tank battalion). A closed position in a closed occupation means that no positions under that occupation (e.g., infantry) are open to women.

[a] All of the Army's closed positions in open occupations are in special forces units and in its Ranger regiment.

[b] Examples of Army occupations that remain closed include infantry, artillery, and armor. This number does not include the combat engineer occupation, as DOD notified Congress of its intent to open this occupation on March 4, 2015.

[c] Examples of Air Force occupations that remain closed include special operations weather (enlisted), combat rescue, and tactical air control party. Air Force occupation data is as of April 30, 2015.

[d] Examples of Navy occupations that remain closed include Navy Sea, Air, and Land (SEALs) and Special Warfare Combatant-Craft Crewmen.

[e] Examples of Marine Corps occupations that remain closed include infantry, artillery, armor, and critical skills operators.

[f] Service positions and occupations that are affiliated with SOCOM are included in the totals listed above for each service; they are also broken out here to show the proportion of closed positions and occupations that are special operations.

[g] Examples of occupations affiliated with SOCOM that remain closed include Navy Sea, Air, and Land (SEALs) and Army Special Forces.

[h] Percentage of closed occupations for SOCOM includes occupations that are only for special operations; it does not include occupations that are also used outside of SOCOM.

Services and SOCOM Permitted to Recommend an Exception to Policy to Keep Positions Closed to Women

As an alternative to opening a position or occupation, the Secretary of Defense has permitted the services to recommend that the Chairman of the Joint Chiefs of Staff and Secretary of Defense approve an exception to policy to keep positions or occupations closed to women.[19] As of May 2015, the Secretary of the Navy was the only military department Secretary to have recommended approval of an exception to policy. The Secretary of the Navy has recommended keeping specific positions closed to the assignment of enlisted women on three classes of ships (frigates, mine countermeasure ships, and patrol coastal craft) that are scheduled to be decommissioned. The rationale for keeping these ship platforms closed to women is in part because they do not have appropriate berthing and because planned decommissioning schedules would mean that modifications would not be a judicious use of resources. Navy officials stated that, while these closed platforms would cause some positions to remain closed to enlisted women, it would not close any occupations to women as there are alternative positions within those occupations on different platforms that are open to women and which provide equal professional opportunity.

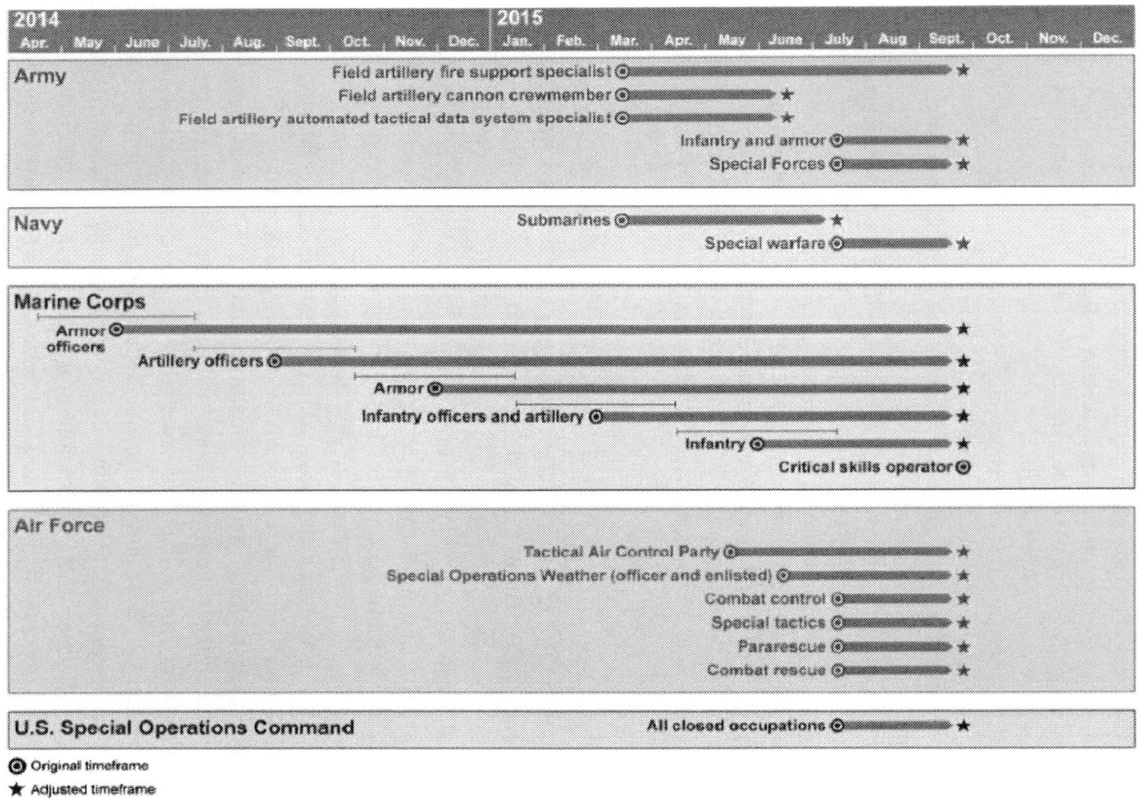

Source: GAO analysis of Department of Defence (DOD) information. | GAO-15-589

Note: These timeframes represent when Secretaries of the military departments will make their recommendations to the Secretary of Defense about whether to open closed positions and occupations. The positions and occupations will not be officially opened to women until DOD subsequently notifies Congress of its intent to open the positions and the waiting period passes.

Figure 3. Changes in Timelines for Military Service and SOCOM Recommendations About Whether to Open Closed Positions and Occupations to Women (as of May 2015).

Issue	Army	Navy	Marine Corps	Air Force	U.S. Special Operations Command
Unit cohesion	✓		✓		✓
Women's health	✓		✓	✓	
Equipment, gear, and uniforms	✓		✓	✓	
Facilities modifications	✓	✓	✓	✓	✓
Interest in serving (propensity)	✓	✓	✓	✓	
International issues	✓		✓		✓

Source: GAO analysis of Department of Defence (DOD) information. | GAO-15-589

Note: Most of the closed Navy and Air Force occupations are associated with SOCOM, and unit cohesion for these positions would be examined under the SOCOM studies.

Figure 4. Areas Where Military Services and SOCOM Are Conducting or Have Conducted Studies to Identify and Mitigate Challenges (as of May 2015).

As of May 2015, none of the other services have requested an exception to keep positions or occupations closed to women or have stated that they plan to request an exception, but the services have all retained the right to request an exception later in the process if they believe there are conditions under which it would be warranted.

Services Are Conducting Studies to Identify Potential Challenges to Integration and Ways to Mitigate These Challenges

The services and SOCOM are conducting studies focused on identifying potential integration challenges and developing ways to mitigate these challenges, as shown in figure 4. The studies address issues such as unit cohesion, women's health, equipment, facilities (e.g., separate restrooms and sleeping quarters), women's interest in serving in ground-combat positions, and international issues. Most of these studies are ongoing, so it is too early to determine the extent to which the services and SOCOM will follow their planned methodologies for identifying challenges and mitigation strategies, or how the services will implement the findings of the studies. See appendix II for a listing of the studies that each service and SOCOM are conducting in their efforts to integrate women.

Unit Cohesion and Military Culture

A common challenge cited in integrating women into previously closed positions and occupations is the potential impact on unit cohesion.[20] Some services are performing studies examining various elements that contribute to unit cohesion. For example, SOCOM, the Army, and the Marine Corps are conducting studies to gauge attitudes toward working with women in integrated units. SOCOM is conducting three studies related to unit cohesion, and SOCOM officials stated that the goal of these studies is to identify potential obstacles and steps to undertake to mitigate those obstacles in an effort to increase their chances of successfully integrating women. For example, SOCOM tasked the RAND Corporation to administer a survey to personnel in closed special operations occupations to discover the attitudes of special operations personnel on the integration of women, including barriers to successful integration and actions to increase the likelihood of success. SOCOM officials stated that initial steps to address concerns raised in the surveys included the Commander of SOCOM holding discussions with his subordinate commanders to provide them information to pass on to their personnel as well as sending an email to all SOCOM personnel to educate the force about what they are doing to validate the standards for special operations positions and why they are validating the standards, and to explain the Joint Staff's guiding principles that govern the integration effort. The first two of the three studies have been completed, and the RAND study is expected to be completed by July 2015.

The Army Research Institute is conducting activities such as surveys, interviews, and focus groups with male and female soldiers assigned to units with newly opened positions and occupations. According to an Army Research Institute official, the institute found that opinions expressed by male soldiers in units assessed at different times since 2012 were less negative a year after female soldiers' integration, and showed a general shift to more neutral and positive perceptions.[21] The official stated that information from these activities is regularly provided to the Army. These activities will likely be conducted until 2018 as additional occupations are opened, according to an Army Research Institute official. As part of its efforts to identify the potential impacts of integration on unit performance, unit cohesion, and unit members' individual interactions, the Marine Corps also is conducting a study through the RAND Corporation. The tasks in this study include a review of literature on integration of women in ground combat and other physically demanding occupations, analysis to identify issues most likely to arise with gender integration of Marine Corps infantry as well as initiatives that might be taken to address them, and development of an approach for monitoring implementation of gender integration of the Marine Corps infantry. This study was scheduled to be completed in March 2015.

Women's Health and Injury Issues

The Marine Corps, the Army, and the Air Force are assessing specific health effects on women when operating in a combat environment. Service officials stated that as women enter direct combat positions, the military will need to make accommodations to address specific health and medical concerns to prevent health problems and to maintain military readiness. For example, the Marine Corps is studying injury prevention and performance enhancement for its training program, including identifying risk factors for injury. This study is scheduled to be completed in August 2015. In addition, according to an Army official, the Army has created a group to review research and data on physical and mental health issues, load carriage,[22] attrition, and performance. Further, the Air Force verified the availability of appropriate medical and psychological support at training locations, and evaluated the medical retention standards for its closed occupations and determined that the existing medical standards were appropriate for both male and female airmen.[23]

Equipment, Gear, and Uniforms

According to officials from the Defense Advisory Committee on Women in the Services, proper combat equipment is essential to overall military readiness; women suffer injuries and do not perform up to their full potential when wearing ill-fitting equipment and combat gear designed for men's bodies. The Marine Corps is conducting a study to identify how adapting equipment design, gear weight, physical fitness composition, or standard operating procedures may support successful completion of required tasks. Marine Corps officials explained that these adaptations could potentially remove impediments to success and thereby enable successful integration. For example, the study may be able to identify alternative methods for loading rounds in armored vehicles so that the task does not require as much upper-body strength. This study is scheduled to be completed by June 30, 2015. Further, according to an Army official, the Army has recently redesigned protective gear items and uniforms with specific fits for female soldiers. In addition, the Air Force has identified training locations that will need female-sized equipment and other equipment such as footgear, clothing, and swimsuits. In June 2015, the Under Secretary of Defense for Acquisition, Technology and Logistics issued guidance directing that the Secretaries of the military departments ensure that combat equipment for female servicemembers is properly designed and fitted, and meets standards for wear and survivability.[24]

Facilities Modifications

The Navy, the Army, the Marine Corps, the Air Force, and the special operations components[25] are assessing the impact on their facilities to integrate women into newly opened positions and occupations. The Navy's proposed Exception to Policy request is based in part on concerns over costs to retrofit the facilities and habitability of three classes of ships (frigates, mine countermeasure ships, and patrol coastal craft) to accommodate women. While many services' facilities are capable of accommodating privacy and berthing needs of women, the services are identifying any changes needed if closed positions are opened to women. For example, if the Army recommends opening its Ranger school to women, the Army may need to make changes to accommodate women into its barracks.[26] Similarly, the Marine Corps is examining potential overall costs to upgrade facilities due to integration requirements, and has projected that costs will be incurred in some buildings due to the need for separate bathrooms and billets, but officials said that the cost will be minimal. The Marine Corps estimated that this effort will be completed in the second quarter of fiscal year 2016. The Air Force also has identified potential facilities changes that would be needed if closed Air Force occupations are opened to women, such as adding or expanding locker rooms for women. Further, all four of the special operations components conducted assessments that determined whether any facilities changes were needed to integrate women.[27]

Women's Interest in Serving in Ground-Combat Positions

All services are studying the propensity (i.e., interest or tendency) of women to serve in selected closed positions and occupations. Officials from the services noted concerns that large numbers of women may not be interested in serving in currently closed ground-combat positions and occupations. Officials from all of the services stated that the integration of women into previously closed positions and occupations would be an asset in finding the best person for the job, and that outreach and recruitment of women for the officer corps is critical to ensuring that our nation's military has the strongest possible leaders. For example, the Marine Corps conducted a study using surveys, market research, available literature and other information to determine the interest of men and women in both the Marine Corps overall and in ground-combat specialties to better understand potential changes in the recruiting market due to the opening of ground-combat arms specialties and units. This study was completed in November 2014.[28] The Army has joined other services in creating advertising campaigns to increase women's interest in selected positions and occupations.[29]

International Issues

SOCOM, the Marine Corps, and the Army are conducting or have conducted international studies analyzing various integration issues. Army Special Operations Command is studying the roles of women to determine how local forces and communities may react to female special forces soldiers. One of the tasks of this study is to provide insights on how the roles of women in different regions and countries may affect the response of local forces and communities to females as Army special forces soldiers. This study is scheduled to be completed before SOCOM is expected to submit its recommendations to the department in September 2015. The Marine Corps also worked with RAND to study other countries with gender-integrated militaries and the practices those countries used for their integration processes. This study was completed in March 2015. According to an Army official, the Army has worked with the U.S. Army Training and Doctrine Command on international comparisons with other countries with integrated armies. This effort was part of the Army's gender-integration study, which is scheduled to be completed in September 2015.

Sexual Assault and Harassment in the Gender-Integration Process

In addition to the challenges reviewed by the services in their studies, we examined the issue of sexual assault and harassment in the integration process. This issue was raised in materials from the Defense Advisory Committee on Women in the Services as a continuing concern related to tracking servicemembers who committed a sex-related offense. According to officials from all services and DOD's Sexual Assault and Prevention Response Office—which has authority, accountability, and oversight of the department's sexual assault prevention and response program—sexual assault and harassment are not inhibitors to the integration of women into previously closed positions and occupations. Officials from all of the services consistently noted that prevention of sexual assault and harassment is a department-wide effort and is not a specific focus of integration efforts. They noted that they consider it to be more of a leadership challenge than an integration challenge. DOD officials said that sexual assault and harassment is not a function of integration and is not gender specific only for women; it affects men and women, and exists in male-only units. In March 2015, we reported that based on survey data, it is estimated that in 2014, about 9,000 to 13,000 male active-duty servicemembers were sexually assaulted, and we also estimated that a much lower percentage of men report their sexual assaults compared to women.[30]

Gender validation requirement	Source	Steps services have taken to satisfy requirement	Army	Navy	Marine Corps	Air Force	SOCOM
1. Ensure gender-neutral evaluation	Statutory requirement[a]	Developing one set of occupational standards for each position	✓	✓	✓	✓	✓
2. Ensure standards reflect job tasks	Statutory requirement[b]	Performing detailed job analysis to identify and define critical physically demanding tasks and the physical abilities needed	✓	✓	✓	✓	✓
		Observing performance of the tasks and surveying subject-matter experts to confirm the specific tasks required for each occupation	✓	✓	✓	✓	✓
3. Validate performance standards	Guiding principles[c]	Conducting studies	✓	✓	✓	✓	✓
4. Ensure eligibility reflects job tasks	Guiding principles[c]	Designing physical task simulations and measures of performance to ensure that simulations are good approximations of job tasks	✓	✓	✓	✓	✓
5. Integrate while preserving readiness, cohesion, and morale	Guiding principles[c]	Efforts will ensure service members in newly opened occupations are able to perform mission and thus maintain readiness	✓	✓	✓	✓	✓
		Conducting studies to determine the potential effect of integration on unit cohesion and identify steps to overcome any obstacles identified	✓		✓		✓

Source: GAO analysis of service and U.S. Special Operations Command (SOCOM) information. | GAO-15-589

Note: Most closed Navy and Air Force occupations are associated with SOCOM, and unit cohesion for these positions would be examined under the SOCOM studies.

[a] National Defense Authorization Act for Fiscal Year 1994, Pub. L. No. 103-160 § 543 (1993), as amended.

[b] Carl Levin and Howard P. "Buck" McKeon National Defense Authorization Act for Fiscal Year 2015, Pub. L. No. 113-291 § 524 (2014).

[c] DOD, memorandum from Chairman of the Joint Chiefs of Staff, *Women in the Service Implementation Plan* (Jan. 9, 2013).

Figure 5. Military Services' Plans to Validate Gender-Neutral Occupational Standards.

Services and SOCOM Have Studies Underway to Validate Gender- Neutral Occupational Standards

The military services and SOCOM are working to address statutory requirements and Joint Staff guidance for validating physically demanding occupational standards by initiating several studies. We identified five elements[31] that the services and SOCOM must address as part of the standards validation process. We compared the five elements to the services' and SOCOM's planned steps and methodologies in their studies and determined that their study plans contained steps that, if carried out as planned, potentially address all five elements, as summarized in figure 5. However, the studies had not yet been completed at the time of our review; therefore, we could not assess the extent to which the studies will follow the planned steps and methodologies or report how results of the studies will be implemented. See appendix II for a complete listing of the planned studies that each service and SOCOM are conducting in their efforts to integrate women.

Ensure Gender-Neutral Evaluation (Statutory Requirement)

The statutory requirements for validating gender-neutral occupational standards direct that any military career designator[32] open to both men and women may not have different standards on the basis of gender.[33] The statute further states that for military career designators where specific physical requirements for muscular strength and endurance and cardiovascular capacity are essential to the performance of duties, those requirements must be applied on a gender-neutral basis. To address this requirement, according to service and SOCOM officials and their respective plans, officials will develop one set of occupational standards for each position that will be applicable to both men and women. One example of this type of effort is the Marine Corps' Ground Combat Element Integrated Task Force, which is to provide the Marine Corps the opportunity to review and refine gender-neutral occupational standards as it evaluates the performance of men and women in integrated units. All of the services' efforts are to be completed by the end of September 2015.

Ensure Standards Reflect Job Tasks (Statutory Requirement)

By statute, the Secretary of Defense must ensure that the gender-neutral occupational standards accurately predict performance of the actual, regular, and recurring job tasks of a military occupation, and are applied equitably to measure individual capabilities.[34] The services' and SOCOM's plans for studies to validate operationally relevant and gender- neutral occupational standards involve identifying the physically demanding tasks required for the specific occupation under study. To address this requirement, all of the services' and SOCOM's plans that we reviewed are taking steps to identify the physically demanding tasks required for each occupation. For example, the Army and the Air Force have undertaken detailed job analyses to identify and define the critical physically demanding tasks and the physical abilities needed to perform them. By observing performance of the tasks and surveying subject- matter experts to confirm the specific tasks required for each occupation, the planned approach intends to confirm that the appropriate tasks have been identified and described. Additionally, the Marine Corps' Ground Combat Element Integrated Task Force plans to quantify tasks, conditions, and standards for job tasks that have previously been qualitative. In March 2015, the Under Secretary of Defense for Personnel and Readiness provided implementing guidance for this statutory requirement,[35] and directed the Secretaries of each military department to provide a written report regarding their validation of individual occupational standards by September 30, 2015,[36] and to require each military department's Inspector General to implement a compliance inspection program to assess whether the services' occupational standards and implementing methodologies are in compliance with statutory requirements.[37]

Validate Performance Standards (Joint Staff Guidance)

Joint Staff guidance directs the services to validate their occupational performance standards. One of the Chairman's guiding principles stated that the services must validate occupational performance standards, both physical and mental, for all military occupational specialties, specifically those that remain closed to women.[38] To address this requirement, all of the services and SOCOM are conducting studies to validate the occupational standards for the positions that have been closed to women. The Army's Training and Doctrine Command and Research Institute of Environmental Medicine are planning to complete by September 2015 the development and validation of gender-neutral occupational testing procedures for entry into the seven military occupational specialties that are closed to women. The Marine Corps opened certain entry-level training schools that previously were closed to women, such as Infantry Training Battalion and Infantry Officer Training,[39] to obtain data on the physical and cognitive/academic demands on female volunteers in these schools. According to Marine Corps officials, this effort will be completed in June 2015. Another Marine Corps effort, projected for completion in June 2015 with a final report by August 2015, is the Ground Combat Element Integrated Task Force.[40] This effort is expected to train female Marine volunteers in skills and tasks performed in closed occupations skills while a dedicated research team observes their performance in both entry-level training and operational environments. Both of these efforts are expected to assist the Marine Corps in validating its standards. In July 2014, the Navy Manpower Analysis Center reviewed all Navy positions to identify those that are physically demanding, and independently reviewed and updated occupational standards for all positions to ensure gender neutrality. The Air Force Air Education and Training Command is planning to complete by July 2015 a study that analyzes and validates physical tests and standards on Battlefield Airmen career fields. A second Air Force study is expected to revalidate physical and mental occupational entry standards across specialties; this study is expected to be completed in September 2015. The special operations components—the Army Special Operations Command, Naval Special Warfare Command, Marine Corps Special Operations Command, and Air Force Special Operations Command—are validating standards for those military occupational specialties that deploy with SOCOM; this is expected to be completed by the end of July 2015.

Ensure Eligibility Reflects Job Tasks (Joint Staff Guidance)

The Chairman's guiding principles also require that eligibility for training and development within designated occupational fields consist of qualitative and quantifiable standards reflecting the knowledge, skills, and abilities necessary for each occupation. To address this requirement, the services and SOCOM have planned studies that aim to validate and select tests to ensure the tests are measuring what they intend to. Further, these plans aim to ensure that scores or results from a test can be used to select individuals for a particular occupation or task. For example, the Air Force is designing physical task simulations, such as climbing a ladder (to simulate entering and exiting a helicopter, according to officials) and lifting and holding objects at different heights (to simulate holding an item to bolt onto an airframe, according to officials). These planned measures of performance are intended to ensure that simulations are good approximations of job tasks. Air Force officials explained that the Air Force's planned approach is to use the operationally-relevant, occupationally-specific critical tasks it identifies as the anchor to develop appropriate physical tests and standards to evaluate the ability to successfully perform operational requirements. This study is expected to be completed by the end of fiscal year 2015.

Integrate While Preserving Readiness, Cohesion, and Morale (Joint Staff Guidance)

Another Chairman's guiding principle requires the services to take action to ensure the success of the warfighting forces by preserving unit readiness, cohesion, and morale. To address this requirement, the services and SOCOM are taking steps to ensure that the integration of women maintains readiness. For example, officials from each of the services stated that the standards-validation efforts will ensure that service members in newly opened occupations are able to perform the mission and thus maintain readiness, operational capability, and combat effectiveness. By observing performance of the tasks and surveying subject-matter experts to confirm that specific tasks are required for each occupation, the services and special operations components plan to confirm those specific tasks that are required for each occupation. Further, as discussed earlier, the Army, Marine Corps, and SOCOM are conducting studies to determine the potential effect of integration on unit cohesion.[41] According to the Defense Advisory Committee on Women in the Services, a common challenge cited in integrating women into previously closed positions and occupations is the potential effect on unit cohesion. Unit cohesion contributes to strong morale and commitment to a mission. By taking steps to identify and address challenges related to unit cohesion, these services are working to ensure that readiness is maintained throughout the integration process.

DOD Is Providing Oversight of Integration Efforts, but Has Not Developed Plans to Monitor Long-Term Progress in Integrating Women into Combat Positions

DOD has been tracking, monitoring, and providing oversight over the services' and SOCOM's efforts to integrate women into ground-combat positions, but has not developed plans to monitor long-term integration progress. Service requests for an exception to policy to keep positions closed to women receive attention from the Chairman of the Joint Chiefs of Staff and the Secretary of Defense. OUSD(P&R) and Joint Staff manage the statutorily required congressional notification process, which is part of a longer process before women can begin serving in newly opened positions and occupations.

OUSD(P&R) and Joint Staff Have Taken Actions to Oversee Services' and SOCOM's Integration Efforts

To oversee the services' and SOCOM's efforts to integrate women into combat positions, OUSD(P&R) and the Chairman of the Joint Chiefs of Staff have issued guidance, commissioned studies, and facilitated coordination and communication through regular meetings among the services and SOCOM. The Secretary of Defense's memorandum rescinding the 1994 rule directed the military departments to submit implementation plans and quarterly progress reports to the Chairman of the Joint Chiefs of Staff and to the Under Secretary of Defense for Personnel and Readiness.[42] Further, Standards for Internal Control in the Federal Government states that ongoing monitoring should be performed continually in the course of normal operations, and should include regular management and supervisory activities, separate evaluations, and policies and procedures to ensure that findings of reviews are promptly resolved.[43]

Both OUSD(P&R) and the Chairman of the Joint Chiefs of Staff have issued guidance to facilitate their efforts to track, monitor, and provide oversight over the services' integration efforts.[44] For example, in January 2013, the Chairman of the Joint Chiefs of Staff issued guidance that established goals and milestones for the services' integration efforts—including validation of gender-neutral occupational standards by September 2015, completion of all studies by the first quarter of fiscal year 2016, and periodic updates in each quarter—and that also established five guiding principles to successfully integrate women into the remaining closed occupational fields.[45] In addition, in February 2013, the Under Secretary of Defense for Personnel and Readiness issued a memorandum directing that quarterly progress reports contain information such as progress on positions that will be opened to women and that are still being evaluated, an assessment of positions that have already been opened, and the development status of gender-neutral occupational standards.[46] An OUSD(P&R) official stated that when reviewing these reports as part of its normal oversight process, OUSD(P&R) has discussed with the services topics such as past and upcoming milestones, recommendation timelines, and the status and progress of ongoing studies. A Joint Staff official explained that the reports are reviewed to ensure progress is being made in accordance with the services' implementation plans. After the reports are reviewed by OUSD(P&R) and Joint Staff, the Chairman provides these reports to the Secretary of Defense.

Further, to help in its oversight of the services' and SOCOM's standards validation efforts, OUSD(P&R) tasked the RAND Corporation to conduct a study concerning validation of gender-neutral occupational standards within the services and SOCOM; an OUSD(P&R) official stated that the study will provide an independent analysis of the services' efforts to validate standards. The first objective of the RAND study is to describe best-practice methodologies for establishing gender-neutral standards for physically demanding jobs, tailored to address the needs of the military.[47] The second objective is to review and evaluate the methodologies used by the services to set gender-neutral standards. In September 2013, RAND issued a draft report addressing the first objective; an OUSD(P&R) official stated that OUSD(P&R) provided a draft of this report to all of the services. In June 2015, RAND officials said that a draft of the second report, which will cover both objectives, is forthcoming.

Moreover, OUSD(P&R) has regular quarterly meetings with the services to discuss topics such as developing the quarterly reports and how others are handling any issues with integration. The Joint Staff also has a meeting process with two different levels of meetings devoted solely to integration efforts: (1) a Joint Chiefs of Staff (four-star level) group, and (2) an Operations Deputies (three-star level) group. A Joint Staff official explained that these meetings provide a forum for the services to share implementation updates, discuss potential barriers, and highlight issues.

The meetings occur at least once every quarter, but can occur more often if needed. OUSD(P&R) and Joint Staff officials stated that there are also frequent communications by other means for the same purposes. For example, in September 2014, SOCOM hosted a workshop for all of the services to review the standards validation process for special operations and the services. SOCOM officials stated that the purpose of this workshop was to ensure that all the services were using similar processes, that no one was working at cross purposes, and that there was no duplication of effort. Officials stated that a follow-up workshop was held in May 2015.

Requests for Exceptions to Policy Receive High- Level Management Attention

The Secretary of Defense and Chairman of the Joint Chiefs of Staff directed that any recommendation for an exception to policy to keep an occupation or position closed to women must be personally approved first by the Chairman and then by the Secretary of Defense.[48] The memorandum states that this approval authority may not be delegated. OUSD(P&R) and Joint Staff officials explained that before such requests are submitted to the Chairman, they are first reviewed for sufficiency by OUSD(P&R) and the Joint Staff. When reviewing any requests for an exception to policy to keep positions closed to women, the Secretary of Defense's January 2013 memorandum states that "[e]xceptions must be narrowly tailored and based on a rigorous analysis of factual data regarding the knowledge, skills and abilities needed for the position."[49] According to OUSD(P&R) and Joint Staff officials, if an exception to policy is requested, they will request all related supporting data and studies and review the request considering all of the factors involved. They stated that once they are satisfied that the Secretary's criteria have been met, they will present the request to the Chairman and then the Secretary to determine whether the request meets the criteria for an exception. According to OUSD(P&R) and Joint Staff officials, they made a conscious decision not to provide or develop specific additional criteria or a format for exception to policy requests—beyond the guidance in the Secretary's memorandum—because they did not want it to appear that there was a checklist for requesting an exception to policy.

When OUSD(P&R) and Joint Staff first reviewed the Navy's July 2014 exception to policy request for the three different ship classes, they jointly requested additional information from the Navy, such as actual modification costs to enable the ships to provide berths for women, officer assignment information, and information on the professional development impact if women do not serve on those ships. An OUSD(P&R) official explained that OUSD(P&R) and Joint Staff worked with the Navy so the Navy would better understand the additional analytical rigor being requested, and they established a deadline for the Navy to provide the requested information in February 2015. The Navy submitted the requested information, and as of April 2015, OUSD(P&R) and Joint Staff officials said the exception to policy request was under review by the Chairman of the Joint Chiefs of Staff, who will then forward his recommendation to the Secretary of Defense.

SOCOM's status as an operational command results in a slightly different process for any exception requests for positions associated with SOCOM. SOCOM officials explained that for any positions associated with SOCOM— whether there is a recommendation to open a position or a request for an exception to policy to keep a position closed to women— there are two recommendations provided. One recommendation comes from the position's parent department Secretary. The second recommendation comes from the SOCOM Commander, and since SOCOM is not a military service that recommendation is then reviewed and approved by the Assistant Secretary of Defense for Special Operations and Low-Intensity Conflict, who serves a military department secretary function for SOCOM. The officials stated that to date there have not been differences between the recommendations from the services and from SOCOM. SOCOM officials explained that there is regular collaboration with the services about recommendations, but that in the event that there was a difference in the two recommendations, the Secretary of Defense would make the decision.

OUSD(P&R) Has Not Developed Plans to Monitor the Services' Progress in Integrating Women into Newly Opened Positions and Occupations after January 2016

As of May 2015, OUSD(P&R) had not developed plans for a mechanism or process to monitor the services' progress in their efforts to integrate newly opened positions and occupations after January 1, 2016. As noted earlier, Standards for Internal Control in the Federal Government states that ongoing monitoring should be performed continually in the course of normal operations.[50] An OUSD(P&R) official stated that OUSD(P&R) will continue to provide oversight as part of its normal responsibilities, and make associated changes in applicable DOD guidance. Further, as discussed earlier, the Under Secretary of Defense for Personnel and Readiness issued guidance that directed each military department to report on its validation of occupational standards, and to implement an inspection program to assess whether the services' occupational standards comply with statutory requirements.[51] However, according to an OUSD(P&R) official, that office does not envision undertaking a formal role in the implementation of the services' recommendations to open closed positions following January 2016.

Further, a Joint Staff official stated that an initial Joint Staff meeting would be held after the January 1, 2016 announcement, and it would be determined at that time whether any additional meetings would be held. OUSD(P&R)'s requirement for the services to submit quarterly progress reports ends in January 2016, and the services have varying plans to monitor implementation after that date. For example, Army officials stated that they have developed an implementation and follow-up plan for beyond 2016 that is being reviewed by senior leaders. Marine Corps officials explained that they have long-term research that will track integration of females, to help understand and shape institutional and individual success, while Navy officials explained that they had not developed any plans to monitor implementation after 2016 and were waiting for direction from OUSD(P&R). However, OUSD(P&R) and Joint Staff officials did not identify any plans to provide such direction for the services to monitor implementation.

After the decisions have been made to open positions and occupations to women, there is a lengthy implementation process before women will be able to serve in the newly opened occupations. Officials from all of the services and SOCOM stated that before women can serve in newly opened positions and occupations they must first be recruited, accessioned, trained, tested, and assigned. As an example of the time involved in just one part of the implementation process, according to OUSD(P&R) officials, the general training timelines can vary by service and the position and occupation, but typically may require less than half a year to almost two years to complete the training part of the implementation process. Without ongoing monitoring of the services' and SOCOM's implementation progress in integrating previously closed positions and occupations, it will be difficult for DOD to have visibility over the extent to which the services and SOCOM are overcoming potential obstacles to integration and DOD will not have information for congressional decision makers about the department's integration progress.

OUSD(P&R) and Joint Staff Manage Congressional Notification Process

OUSD(P&R) and Joint Staff manage the congressional notification process when positions and occupations are being opened to women. By statute, the Secretary of Defense must provide Congress with a report prior to implementing any proposed changes that would result in opening or closing any category of unit or position, or military career designator to women.[52] As part of the process for opening formerly closed positions and occupations, an OUSD(P&R) official explained that OUSD(P&R) analyzes information provided by the military department secretaries and the Assistant Secretary of Defense for Special Operations and Low- Intensity Conflict[53] and verifies items such as the correct occupational specialties (if applicable), that all appropriate additional skill identifiers are included, and that the correct number of positions to be opened is reflected. OUSD(P&R) officials then create a packet to send to Congress after they prebrief the House and Senate Armed Services Committees. A Joint Staff official stated that Joint Staff also reviews the notifications, and provides comments on the briefings given to Congress.

In the congressional notifications of the department's intent to open positions and occupations to women, DOD is required to provide a detailed legal analysis regarding the legal implications of the proposed change with respect to the constitutionality of the application of the 1948 Military Selective Service Act[54] to males only.[55] This act empowers the President to require the registration of every male citizen and resident alien between the ages of 18 and 26.[56] In 1981, the Supreme Court upheld the constitutionality of the male-only registration requirement.[57] Currently, women serve voluntarily in the U.S. armed forces, but are not required to register with the Selective Service and would not be subject to a draft. DOD's legal analyses in the congressional notifications submitted since January 2013 have not found that opening the positions and occupations to women would affect the constitutionality of the act. Officials from OUSD(P&R), the services, and the Defense Advisory Committee on Women in the Services have stated that if DOD decides to open ground-combat occupations such as infantry, artillery, and armor, DOD's required legal analysis could raise concerns about the constitutionality of the act. DOD's legal analysis in the March 2015 congressional notification to open the Army combat engineer occupation stated that "[o]ver time, however, the opening of additional combat positions to women may further alter the factual backdrop to the Court's decision in Rostker. Should the constitutionality of the

[Military Selective Service Act] be challenged at a later date, the reasoning behind the exclusion of women from registration may need to be reexamined." An OUSD(P&R) official explained that even if DOD's legal analysis raises constitutionality concerns about the act, DOD could still submit the notification to Congress and take actions to implement opening those positions to women after completion of the waiting period.

After a notification is provided to Congress, the Secretary of Defense is prohibited from implementing any proposed changes until "after the end of a period of 30 days of continuous session of Congress (excluding any day on which either house of Congress is not in session) following the date on which the report is received."[58] This waiting period allows Congress time to take any legislative actions that it deems necessary based on the notification and report provided by DOD. However, the congressional calendar has resulted in an average time period of about 90 calendar days before planned changes could be implemented; three of the twelve congressional notifications DOD submitted between April 2013 and July 2014 have taken almost 5 months.[59] After the waiting period has passed, OUSD(P&R) notifies the appropriate elements within a service so that they can begin implementing actions to open the positions. Since the services are allowed to take actions to open positions only after the waiting period is over, Army and Navy officials said that the delays and unpredictability associated with the waiting period pose challenges in beginning the recruiting, accession, and training processes, and aligning assignments to newly opened positions with service promotion cycles. An OUSD(P&R) official stated that in 2014 DOD was requested to provide drafting assistance on a legislative proposal for a change that would have modified the waiting period from 30 days of continuous session of Congress to 60 calendar days, but said that Congress did not act at that time.

In 2012, we assessed the military necessity of the Selective Service System and examined alternatives to its current structure.[60] We found that because of its reliance and emphasis on the All Volunteer Force, DOD had not reevaluated requirements for the Selective Service System since 1994, even though the national security environment had changed significantly since that time. The registration system in fiscal year 2014 had an annual budget of $22.9 million;[61] DOD officials stated that the system provides a low-cost insurance policy in case a draft is ever necessary. In our 2012 report, we recommended that DOD (1) evaluate DOD's requirements for the Selective Service System in light of recent strategic guidance and report the results to Congress; and (2) establish a process of periodically reevaluating DOD's requirements for the Selective Service System in light of changing threats, operating environments, and strategic guidance.

In responding to these recommendations, DOD stated in February 2013 that there was no longer an immediate military necessity for the Selective Service System, but there was a national necessity because the registration process provides the structure for mobilization that would allow the services to rapidly increase in size if needed. DOD's assessment was limited to a reevaluation of mission and military necessity for the Selective Service System. Regarding the second recommendation, DOD had not taken action as of June 2015, but agreed that a thorough assessment of the issue was merited, and should include a review of the statutes and policies surrounding the current registration process and the potential to include the registration of women. However, DOD officials stated that such a review should be part of a broader national discussion and should not be determined only by DOD.[62] As we noted in our 2012 report, a reevaluation of the department's personnel needs for the Selective Service System in light of current national security plans would better position Congress to make an informed decision about the necessity of the Selective Service System or any other alternatives that might substitute for it. For example, a 2013 Congressional Research Service report noted the Selective Service issue could become moot by terminating Selective Service registration or expanding registration requirements to include women.[63] We agree that this is a broader issue. DOD is the agency that would use the Selective Service System in the event a draft was needed. Thus, we continue to believe that our 2012 recommendation has merit—that DOD should take the lead in conducting an evaluation of requirements for the Selective Service System and should establish a process of periodically reevaluating DOD's requirements for the Selective Service System in light of changing threats, operating environments, and strategic guidance.

CONCLUSION

The Secretary of Defense and the Chairman of the Joint Chiefs of Staff have ordered that women, to the extent possible, be integrated into direct ground-combat positions and occupations by January 2016. Although OUSD(P&R) and Joint Staff have been tracking, monitoring, and providing oversight of the services' and SOCOM's integration efforts, they do not have plans to monitor the services' implementation progress after January 2016, as newly opened positions are integrated. Without ongoing monitoring of the services' and SOCOM's progress in integrating previously closed positions and occupations after January 2016, it will be difficult for DOD to have visibility over the extent that the services and SOCOM are overcoming potential obstacles to integration and DOD may not be able to provide current information for congressional decision makers about the department's progress. Further, DOD has not established a process to reevaluate its requirements for the Selective Service System that could enable it to take into account these changes in expanding combat service opportunities for women. If DOD conducted a comprehensive reevaluation of the department's personnel needs for the Selective Service System, the analysis would better position Congress to make an informed decision about the necessity of the Selective Service System or any other alternatives that might substitute for it.

Recommendation for Executive Action

To help ensure successful integration of combat positions that have been opened to women, we recommend that the Secretary of Defense direct the Under Secretary of Defense for Personnel and Readiness to develop plans for monitoring after January 2016 the services' implementation of their integration efforts and progress in opening positions to women, including an approach for taking any needed action.

Agency Comments

We provided a draft of this report to DOD for review and comment. In written comments, DOD concurred with our recommendation. DOD noted that they recognize the importance of monitoring long-term implementation progress of expanding combat service opportunities for women. DOD also provided technical comments, which we have incorporated in the report where appropriate.

Brenda S. Farrell
Director, Defense Capabilities and Management

APPENDIX I: SCOPE AND METHODOLOGY

This report assesses the Department of Defense's (DOD) efforts to expand combat service opportunities for women. Our scope included efforts of the four military services in DOD and U.S. Special Operations Command (SOCOM) since January 2013, when the Secretary of Defense eliminated the prohibition on women serving in combat positions. We did not include the Coast Guard in our review. Table 3 contains a list of the agencies we contacted during our review.

Table 3. Agencies Contacted during Review

Office of the Secretary of Defense	Office of the Undersecretary of Defense, Personnel and Readiness
	Office of the Undersecretary of Defense, Special Operations and Low IntensityConflict
Joint Chiefs of Staff	Joint Staff, Personnel and Readiness Division
Department of the Army	Command Policy Division Directorate Military Personnel Management
	Training and Doctrine Command
	Army Research Institute for the Behavioral and Social Sciences
Department of the Air Force	Air Force Assignments and Women in Service Review Branch office
	Air Education and Training Command
	Accessions and Training Division
Department of the Navy	Navy Office of Women's Policy
	Enlisted Women in Submarines Task Force
	Navy Education Training Command
	Naval Health Research Center
	Navy Manpower Analysis Center
U.S. Marine Corps	Marine Corps Force Innovation Office
	Operations Analysis Division
	Marine Corps Operational Test and Evaluation Activity
	Marine Corps Training and Education Command
U.S. Special Operations Command	Special Operations Command Women in Service Review Office
	Army Special Operations Command
	Marine Corps Special Operations Command
	Naval Special Warfare Command
Defense Advisory Committee on Women in the Services	
Sexual Assault Prevention and Response Office	
RAND Corporation	

Source: GAO. | GAO-15-589

To determine the status of service efforts to open previously closed positions and occupations and the extent potential challenges have been identified and mitigated, we analyzed documentation and spoke with officials to identify the positions and occupations that have been opened to women, that remain closed, timeframes for making decisions, whether any services planned to keep any positions or occupations closed to women, and any steps taken to identify potential challenges and develop approaches to overcome any such challenges. Specifically, we reviewed guidance provided to the services from the Secretary of Defense,[64] the Chairman of the Joint Chiefs of Staff,[65] and the Under Secretary of Defense for Personnel and Readiness[66] to determine what the services were required to do as part of their efforts to determine whether to open closed positions and occupations to women. We determined that the services were required to, among other things, develop implementation plans, follow five guiding principles when opening positions and occupations to women, and create and submit quarterly progress reports starting in the third quarter of fiscal year 2013. At the department level, the military departments were required to submit detailed implementation plans consistent with the guiding principles and goals and milestones provided by the Chairman.[67]

To determine whether the services and SOCOM met these requirements, we obtained and analyzed the services' and SOCOM's respective implementation plans, quarterly progress reports, congressional notifications, and Navy exception to policy documents, and discussed these documents with officials from the services, SOCOM, and the Office of the Under Secretary of Defense for Personnel and Readiness (OUSD(P&R)). To determine if the services and SOCOM met all of the implementation plan requirements, we analyzed the services' and SOCOM's implementation plans for required components—such as timelines and timeframes for opening positions and occupations to women, milestones for development of gender-neutral occupational standards, and consistency with the guiding principles. To determine if the services and SOCOM met all of the quarterly progress report requirements, we analyzed the quarterly and bi-annual reports for required components—such as updates on assessments and progress on positions that are slated for opening or currently being evaluated, analysis of any request for an exception to policy, discussion regarding the development status of gender-neutral standards, assessments of newly opened positions, identification of any limiting factors, and recommendations for additional openings. We analyzed how some of the timeframes changed through quarterly report progress updates and interviews with service officials, by comparing them to the original ones set in the implementation plans. To determine what positions and occupations had been opened to women since January 2013, we analyzed the congressional notifications that DOD had provided to Congress from January 2013 through March 2015, and discussed this data with officials from the services and OUSD(P&R).

To determine what positions and occupations remain closed to women and to determine the services' and SOCOM's timeframes for making decisions about whether to open these positions and occupations to women, we analyzed the services' and SOCOM's implementation plans, and quarterly and biannual progress reports and interviewed officials from the services, SOCOM, and OUSD(P&R). In addition, we requested and obtained data from the services and SOCOM on the total number of positions and occupations closed to women as of March 2015, as well as the total number of positions and occupations in each service and in SOCOM. We analyzed the reliability of this data by obtaining information on how the data were collected, managed, and used through interviews with and questionnaires to relevant officials and by reviewing supporting documentation. To corroborate this data, we cross-referenced it with documentation on closed positions and occupations provided by OUSD(P&R), as well as similar data provided by the services and SOCOM in their progress reports. This data was also verified by officials from OUSD(P&R), the services, and SOCOM. Although we found some discrepancies in some of the data regarding the number of closed positions reported by the services, which officials explained were due in part to changes in force structure, we determined that the data were sufficiently reliable to report on the general number and percentage of positions and occupations that are closed to women in each of the services and in SOCOM.

To determine any steps that DOD and the services took to identify potential challenges and develop approaches to overcome any such challenges, we analyzed service and SOCOM implementation plans, quarterly reports, and studies and study documentation. We also interviewed officials at OUSD(P&R), Joint Staff, Defense Advisory Committee on Women in the Services, Sexual Assault Prevention and Response Office, and within each of the services and SOCOM, and discussed potential challenges they have identified and approaches to mitigating these challenges. In inquiring about challenges, we asked about challenges in general, as well as specific issues that we had identified in the services' implementation plans, reports by the Defense Advisory Committee on Women in the Services, and prior GAO work as potential areas of study. The specific issues that we asked about were the Military Selective Service Act, women's health, sexual harassment and assault, unit cohesion, facilities issues (e.g., berthing, privacy), promotion and retention, and equipment.

To determine the extent to which service efforts to validate gender-neutral occupational standards are consistent with statutory requirements and Joint Staff guidance, we identified requirements from statutes and Joint Staff guidance and compared these requirements against service plans for studies. To identify the requirements for validating gender-neutral occupational standards, we reviewed relevant laws as well as guidance issued by the Chairman of the Joint Chiefs of Staff. Specifically, to identify statutory requirements, we reviewed the National Defense Authorization Act for Fiscal Year 1994[68] and the Carl Levin and Howard P. "Buck" McKeon National Defense Authorization Act for 2015.[69] To identify Joint Staff guidance, we reviewed the Chairman's January 2013 memorandum that laid out guiding principles for the services to follow in integrating women.[70] From these laws and guidance, we identified five specific elements the services must follow in validating their gender-neutral occupational standards. Two elements are from statutory requirements: (1) ensure gender-neutral evaluation and (2) ensure standards reflect job tasks. Three elements are from Joint Staff guidance: (1) validate performance standards; (2) ensure eligibility reflects job tasks, and (3) integrate while preserving readiness, cohesion, and morale. To determine if the services are following these requirements and guidance, we obtained plans for studies from each of the military services and SOCOM. These plans included descriptions of scope, methodology, and timeframes for completion. We then compared these plans against the requirements we identified to determine if these planned studies met the requirements for validating gender-neutral occupational standards. Two analysts independently reviewed and assessed the plans to determine whether they contain the two statutory elements provided by the National Defense Authorization Act for Fiscal Year 1994, as amended, and the Carl Levin and Howard P. "Buck" McKeon National Defense Authorization Act for Fiscal Year 2015 and the three elements provided by the Chairman's memorandum. The analysts then compared their results to identify any disagreements and reached agreement on all items through discussion. However, the results from these studies are not yet completed; therefore, we could not assess the extent to which the completed studies will follow the planned steps and methodologies or report how results of the studies will be implemented. We also interviewed and discussed these requirements and studies with DOD and service officials, particularly officials involved in conducting these studies.

To determine the extent to which DOD is tracking, monitoring, and providing oversight over the military services' plans to complete the integration of women in direct combat positions by January 2016, we obtained and analyzed documentation and discussed with officials from OUSD(P&R) and Joint Staff the nature and level of their tracking and monitoring, and their review of the military services' and SOCOM's efforts to integrate women into combat positions. Specifically, we assessed OUSD(P&R) and Joint Staff's review of the military services' and SOCOM's implementation plans, and quarterly and biannual progress reports. We then compared these efforts to DOD guidance[71] and internal control standards.[72] Further, we reviewed documentation and discussed with OUSD(P&R) officials a study being performed by the RAND Corporation for OUSD(P&R) as part of their oversight of the services' and SOCOM's efforts to validate gender-neutral occupational standards, and we met with RAND officials to discuss their work on this study. We also obtained and analyzed documentation related to the Navy's request for an exception to policy to keep positions closed on three classes of ships, and we discussed with P&R, Joint Staff, and Navy officials the process and criteria used to review this request.

In assessing the oversight and review of DOD's congressional notifications when positions and occupations are being opened to women, we analyzed the applicable statutory requirements for these congressional notifications,[73] including the requirement to provide a detailed legal analysis of the constitutionality of the 1948 Military Selective Service Act.[74] In addition, we reviewed the Military Selective Service Act, its legislative history,[75] and associated Supreme Court case law.[76] We discussed with DOD and service officials the process for preparing this legal analysis and the extent to which their efforts to open additional positions and occupations to women could affect that legal analysis. We discussed with OUSD(P&R) officials the process for calculating the waiting period and their efforts to modify the statutory timeframe for the waiting period, and obtained data on the amount of time for each waiting period to pass since January 2013. We also analyzed prior reports from GAO,[77] DOD, the Congressional Research Service,[78] the Defense Advisory Committee on Women in the Services,[79] and the Federal Advisory Committee on Gender-Integrated Training and Related Issues to identify changes in statutes and military guidance that have increased opportunities for women to serve in combat roles over the past several decades. We determined changes that have occurred in DOD's workforce and environment over the past several decades and assessed the extent that these changes could have an effect on the utility of the Military Selective Service Act in meeting the department's needs.

We conducted this performance audit from September 2014 to July 2015 in accordance with generally accepted government auditing standards. Those standards require that we plan and perform the audit to obtain sufficient, appropriate evidence to provide a reasonable basis for our findings and conclusions based on our audit objectives. We believe that the evidence obtained provides a reasonable basis for our findings and conclusions based on our audit objectives.

APPENDIX II: SUMMARY OF SERVICE AND SOCOM STUDIES THAT WILL INFORM INTEGRATION RECOMMENDATIONS AND IMPLEMENTATION EFFORTS

Organization Conducting Study	Study	Study Purpose
Office of the Under Secretary of Defense for Personnel and Readiness		
RAND Corporation	1. Defining Physical Standards for Physically Demanding Jobs: A Review of Methods	Identify best practices for validating standards in physically demanding occupations
	2. An Overview of the Services' Current Efforts to Establish Gender Neutral Physical Standards	Assess how the military services and Special Operations Command are aligned with the identified best practices in their respective validation efforts
Department of the Army		
U.S. Army Research Institute of Environmental Medicine	1. Development of Military Occupation-Specific Physical Employment Standards, Study 1	Standards validation
	2. Development of Military Occupation-Specific Physical Employment Standards, Study 2	Standards validation
	3. Development of Military Occupation-Specific Physical Employment Standards, Study 3	Standards validation

Organization Conducting Study	Study	Study Purpose
U.S. Army Research Institute for the Behavioral and Social Sciences	4. Expanded Positions for Women in Open Occupations for the Original Nine Exception to Policy Brigade Combat Teams[a]	Collect data, through surveys, interviews, and focus groups, on perceptions of the assignment of female soldiers serving in specialties open to women in select Brigade Combat Teams
	5. Expanded Positions for Female Soldiers in Open Occupations Assessment for administration with Field Artillery Brigades	Collect data, through surveys, interviews, and focus groups, on perceptions of the impact of the assignment of female soldiers to previously closedpositions in select Field Artillery Brigades
	6. Expanded Positions for Women in Open Occupations in Deployed and National Guard Units	Online surveys with additional Active and National Guard Brigade Combat Teams.
	7. End of Training Assessment for Gender Integration Efforts	Provide assessment of potential issues associatedwith gender integration in newly opened occupations and currently closed occupations to be opened.
Naval Health Research Center	9. Validating Gender-Neutral Standards for U.S. Army Special Operations Command	Standards validation
U.S. Marine Corps		
Operational Test and Evaluation Activity	1. Ground Combat Element Integrated Task Force[b]	The task force will train female Marine volunteers in closed military occupational specialty skills, andintegrate them into a combat arms unit, while a dedicated research team observes the unit's performance in an operational environment
Training and Education Command	2. Collection and Assessment of Training Performance Data at Infantry Officers Course	To collect data on female training performance while undergoing infantry training at Infantry Officers Course
	3. Assessment of Training Performance of Female Enlisted Marines at Infantry Training Battalion	To assess the performance of female enlisted Marine volunteers assigned to the Infantry Training Battalion

(Continued)

Organization Conducting Study	Study	Study Purpose
	4. Assessment of Training Performance of Female Enlisted Marines Volunteers in the Combat Arms (Non-Infantry) Formal Learning Centers	To assess the performance of female enlisted Marine volunteers assigned to the artillery, tank, assault amphibian vehicle courses
Marine Corps Recruiting Command	5. Propensity Analysis	Determine the potential effects of lifting combat exclusion provisions on the propensity to enlist and commission both male and female applicants
Operations Analysis Division	6. Smart Adaptations for the Gender Integrated Marine Corps	Identify potential adaptations for the barriers to success, as well as the associated costs, implementation considerations, operational effectiveness, and the number of Marines potentially impacted
	7. Assessment of Marine Non-Deployability and the Effects of Readiness	Measure and evaluate the effects of non-deployable Marines and evaluate policies regarding non-deployability
	8. Study of Talent, Attrition, Retention, and Success	Multi-purpose research effort that will, among other goals, provide information and analysis concerning the reasons and/or personnel predictors for female officer attrition in the Marine Corps
Naval Health Research Center	9. U.S. Naval Unit Behavioral Health Needs Assessment Survey	Evaluate the behavioral and psychological health of integrated battalions in the Ground Combat Element Integrated Task Force
Center for Naval Analyses	10. Study of historical U.S. Marine Corps integration efforts	Review the integration of women into Marine Corps aviation occupations and past studies on the performance of female Marines in aviation andlogistics.
	11. Ground Combat Element Integrated Task Force surveys, focus	To understand the effects of gender integration into a combat arms units using surveys,

Organization Conducting Study	Study	Study Purpose
	groups and leadership interviews	directed focus groups and leadership interviews to gain perspectives from all Marines
	12. Male and Female Marines' Performance in Aviation and Logistics Occupations	To understand the integration of women into the logistics and aviation communities
	13. Expand Unit Assignments Survey	Determine participants' experiences regarding gender integration in newly-integrated ground combat units particularly with respect to potential effects on readiness, morale, and unit cohesion.
RAND Corporation	14. Key Considerations in Assessing the Impact of Integrating Women into Marine Corps Infantry Units	Determine potential impact of integrating women into Marine Corps military occupational specialties, with a particular focus on the infantry.
University of Pittsburgh	15. Injury Prevention and Performance Enhancement in Army and Marine Personnel	Create a systematic and sustained injury prevention and performance enhancement training program.
Center for Strategic and International Studies	16. Red Team—Evaluating all Marine Corps Research and Assessment	Evaluate the Marine Corps' data collection plan/or the integration of females
Michigan State University	17. Decision-Making Study	To understand potential effects of gender in small team decision-making scenarios
Department of the Navy		
Center for Naval Analyses	1. Support for the Enlisted Women in Submarines Task Force	To build a model that could determine the timeline to sustainability of a proposed integration plan and to determine the effect of the integration plan on the gender mix in the rest of the Navy
Navy Manpower Analysis Center	2. Navy Manpower Analysis Center Periodic Review of Standards	Standards Validation

(Continued)

Organization Conducting Study	Study	Study Purpose
	3. Naval Manpower Analysis Center Review of all Enlisted Occupational Standards and Navy Enlisted Classifications	Determine the most physically demanding ratings and Navy Enlisted Classifications
Naval Health Research Center	4. Naval Special Warfare Standards Validation Study	Evaluating and validating gender-neutral standards for Sea, Air, and Land Teams (SEAL) and Special Warfare Combatant Crewman (SWCC) selection and the underlying physical demands of their operations
Department of the Air Force		
Accessions and Training Division, Air Force Personnel Center with RAND Corporation	1. Initial Qualification Standards Validation Study	Mental and physical entry standards re-validation for all Air Force specialty codes
Air Education and Training Command with RAND Corporation	2. Physical Performance Tests and Standards Validation Study	Physical standards validation for Battlefield occupations for selection, training, and operations
U.S. Special Operations Command		
Joint Special Operations University	1. Special Operations Forces Mixed-Gender Elite Teams	Examine if changing the gender component of small, elite teams would affect team dynamics in a way that would compromise the ability of the team to meet a mission objective.
University of Kansas	2. Project Diane: Barriers and Benefits of Integration	Explore potential barriers and benefits of integrating females into Army Special Forces currently positions closed to females
RAND Corporation	3. Enabling an Efficient and Effective Global Special Operations Forces Network	Assess the range of potential obstacles to effective integration of women into Special Operations Forces, focusing on the unit- and team-level.

Organization Conducting Study	Study	Study Purpose
	4. The Roles of Women in Indigenous Cultures	Assess how indigenous definitions of women's roles could affect the response of local forces and communities to female Army Special Forces soldiers.
U.S. Army Special Operations Command	5. Doctrine, Organization, Training, Material, Leadership, and Education Analysis	Identify impacts, evaluate psychological and socialconsiderations, and review gender neutral standards that may be impacted by opening all Army Special Operations Command occupations and positions to women.
U. S. Marine Corps Forces Special Operations Command	6. Doctrine, Organization, Training, Material, Leadership, and Education Analysis	Identify impacts, evaluate psychological and socialconsiderations, and review gender neutral standards that may be impacted by opening all Marine Corps Forces Special Operations Command occupations and positions to women.
Naval Special Warfare Command	7. Doctrine, Organization, Training, Material, Leadership, and Education Analysis	Identify impacts, evaluate psychological and socialconsiderations, and review gender neutral standards that may be impacted by opening all Naval Special Warfare occupations and positions to women.
U.S. Air Force Special Operations Command	8. Doctrine, Organization, Training, Material, Leadership, and Education Analysis	Identify impacts, evaluate psychological and socialconsiderations, and review gender neutral standards that may be impacted by opening all Air Force Special Operations Command occupations and positions to women.

Source: GAO analysis of DOD information. | GAO-15-589.

[a] In 2012, DOD approved an exception to the Direct Ground Combat Assignment Rule Policy for the Army, and enabled the Army to assign women to enlisted and officer positions at the battalion level in open occupations in nine Brigade Combat Teams.

[b] George Mason University is providing a peer review of the Ground Combat Element Integrated Task Force.

Related GAO Products

Military Personnel: DOD Has Taken Steps to Meet the Health Needs of Deployed Servicewomen, but Actions Are Needed to Enhance Care for Sexual Assault Victims. GAO-13-182. Washington, D.C.: January 29, 2013.

National Security: DOD Should Reevaluate Requirements for the Selective Service System. GAO-12-623. Washington, D.C.: June 7, 2012.

Gender Issues: Trends in the Occupational Distribution of Military Women. GAO/NSIAD-99-212. Washington, D.C.: September 14, 1999.

Gender Issues: Perceptions of Readiness in Selected Units. GAO/NSIAD-99-120. Washington, D.C.: May 13, 1999.

Gender Issues: Information to Assess Servicemembers' Perceptions of Gender Inequities Is Incomplete. GAO/NSIAD-99-27. Washington, D.C.: November 18, 1998.

Gender Issues: Improved Guidance and Oversight Are Needed to Ensure Validity and Equity of Fitness Standards. GAO/NSIAD-99-9. Washington, D.C.: November 17, 1998.

Gender Issues: Information on DOD's Assignment Policy and Direct Ground Combat Definition. GAO/NSIAD-99-7. Washington, D.C.: October 19, 1998.

Gender Issues: Changes Would Be Needed to Expand Selective Service Registration to Women. GAO/NSIAD-98-199. Washington, D.C.: June 30, 1998.

Gender Issues: Analysis of Methodologies in Reports to the Secretaries of Defense and the Army. GAO/NSIAD-98-125. Washington, D.C.: March 16, 1998.

Selective Service: Cost and Implications of Two Alternatives to the Present System. GAO/NSIAD-97-225. Washington, D.C.: September 10, 1997.

Gender Integration in Basic Training: The Services Are Using a Variety of Approaches. GAO/T-NSIAD-97-174. Washington, D.C.: June 5, 1997.

Physically Demanding Jobs: Services Have Little Data on Ability of Personnel to Perform. GAO/NSIAD-96-169. Washington, D.C.: July 9, 1996.

Basic Training: Services Are Using a Variety of Approaches to Gender Integration. GAO/NSIAD-96-153. Washington, D.C.: June 10, 1996.

Women in the Military: Deployment in the Persian Gulf War. GAO/NSIAD-93-93. Washington, D.C.: July 13, 1993.

Women in the Military: Air Force Revises Job Availability but Entry Screening Needs Review. GAO/NSIAD-91-199. Washington, D.C.: August 30, 1991.

Women in the Military: More Military Jobs Can Be Opened Under Current Statutes. GAO/NSIAD-88-222. September 7, 1988.

Women in the Military: Impact of Proposed Legislation to Open More Combat Support Positions and Units to Women. GAO/NSIAD-88-197BR. Washington, D.C.: July 15, 1988.

Combat Exclusion Laws for Women in the Military. GAO/T-NSIAD-88-8. Washington, D.C.: November 19, 1987.

End Notes

[1] A Department of Defense (DOD) memorandum entitled *Direct Ground Combat Definition and Assignment Rule* (Jan. 13, 1994) prohibited the assignment of women to positions in units below the brigade level whose primary mission is to engage in direct combat on the ground. The memorandum permitted additional restrictions on several additional bases, and allowed the services to propose further restrictions on the assignment of women, together with justification for those proposed restrictions.

[2] DOD, memorandum from Secretary of Defense and Chairman of the Joint Chiefs of Staff, *Elimination of the 1994 Direct Ground Combat Definition and Assignment Rule* (Jan. 24, 2013). This memorandum requires that the integration of women into newly opened positions and units occur as expeditiously as possible, considering good order and judicious use of fiscal resources, but must be completed no later than January 1, 2016.The memorandum also requires that any recommendation to keep an occupational specialty or unit closed to women must be personally approved first by the Chairman of the Joint Chiefs of Staff, and then by the Secretary of Defense. Any exceptions must also be narrowly tailored, and based on a rigorous analysis of factual data regarding the knowledge, skills and abilities needed for the position.

[3] Senate Report No. 113-176, at 116-117 (2014), which accompanied S. 2410, a proposed bill for the National Defense Authorization Act for Fiscal Year 2015.

[4] For purposes of this report, we use the terms military services or services when we are referring to the Air Force, the Army, the Marine Corps, and the Navy.

[5] SOCOM is a functional combatant command responsible for programming, budgeting, acquisition, training, organizing, equipping, and providing special operations forces and developing special operations forces strategy, doctrine, tactics, and procedures. SOCOM activities include counterterrorism operations, counterproliferation of weapons of mass destruction, security force assistance, counterinsurgency, and special reconnaissance, among others. SOCOM forces are active and reserve forces of the military services that are specifically organized, trained, and equipped to conduct and support special operations.

[6] Carl Levin and Howard P. "Buck" McKeon National Defense Authorization Act for Fiscal Year 2015, Pub. L. No. 113-291 § 524(a) (2014); National Defense Authorization Act for Fiscal Year 1994, Pub. L. No. 103-160 § 543 (1993), as amended by the National Defense Authorization Act for Fiscal Year 2014, Pub. L. No. 113-66 § 523 (2013).

[7] DOD, memorandum from the Chairman of the Joint Chiefs of Staff, *Women in the Service Implementation Plan* (Jan. 9, 2013).

[8] DOD, memorandum from the Chairman of the Joint Chiefs of Staff, *Women in the Service Implementation Plan* (Jan. 9, 2013); Memorandum from the Under Secretary of Defense for Personnel and Readiness, *Elimination of the 1994 Direct Ground Combat Definition and Assignment Rule* (Feb. 27, 2013).

[9] Pub. L. No. 80-625, 62 Stat. 356-75 (June 12, 1948).

[10] DOD memorandum, *Direct Ground Combat Definition and Assignment Rule* (Jan. 13, 1994).

[11] Direct ground combat was defined as "engaging an enemy on the ground with individual or crew-served weapons, while being exposed to hostile fire and to a high probability of direct physical contact with the hostile force's personnel. Direct ground combat takes place well forward on the battlefield while locating and closing with the enemy to defeat them by fire, maneuver, or shock effect."

[12] DOD, Office of the Under Secretary of Defense for Personnel and Readiness, *Report to Congress on the Review of Laws, Policies and Regulations Restricting the Service of Female Members in the U.S. Armed Forces* (February 2012).

[13] At the time of DOD's report, only the Army had designated restricted positions based solely on the co-location criterion.

[14] DOD, Office of the Under Secretary of Defense Personnel and Readiness, *Report to Congress on Women in the Services Review* (July 2013).

[15] National Defense Authorization Act for Fiscal Year 1994, Pub. L. No. 103-160 § 543 (1993), as amended by Pub. L. No. 113-66 § 523 (2013) (appended as a note below 10 U.S.C. § 113).

[16] More than 99 percent of the Air Force's occupations were open to women as of January 2013.

[17] There are two types of positions that are closed to women in the services and SOCOM. The first is a closed position in a closed occupation, meaning no positions under that occupation (e.g., infantry) are open to women. The second is a closed position in an open occupation, meaning that while the occupation is open to women, specific positions within certain units are closed to women (e.g., administration clerk in a tank battalion).

[18] DOD, memorandum from the Secretary of Defense and Chairman of the Joint Chiefs of Staff, *Elimination of the 1994 Direct Ground Combat Definition and Assignment Rule* (Jan. 24, 2013). The Chairman and Under Secretary of Defense for Personnel and Readiness provided further guidance on the content of the quarterly progress reports. See DOD, memorandum from the Chairman of the Joint Chiefs of Staff, *Women in the Service Implementation Plan* (Jan. 9, 2013); and DOD, memorandum from the Under Secretary of Defense for Personnel and Readiness, *Elimination of the 1994 Direct Ground Combat Definition and Assignment Rule* (Feb. 27, 2013).

[19] This option was included in the January 24, 2013, memo where the Secretary of Defense and the Chairman of the Joint Chiefs of Staff rescinded the 1994 rule restricting women from serving in direct ground-combat positions.

[20] For example, The RAND Corporation—a nonprofit institution whose mission is to help improve policy and decision making through research and analysis—has reported that unit cohesion is built through propinquity (meaning people who happen to be around us), shared group membership, attitude similarity, success experiences, shared threat, and leadership and training. See RAND National Defense Research Institute, *Sexual Orientation and U.S. Military Personnel Policy: An Update of RAND's 1993 Study* (2010). RAND's report distinguishes between two types of cohesion—task cohesion and social— to better analyze how interpersonal dynamics affect performance of small organizations such as military units. Task cohesion is defined as the shared commitment among members to achieving a goal that requires the collective efforts of the group. A group with high task cohesion is composed of members who share a common goal and who are motivated to coordinate their efforts as a team to achieve that goal. Social cohesion is the extent that group members like each other, prefer to spend their social time together, enjoy each other's company, and feel emotionally close to one another.

[21] We did not review or assess the validity of these survey results because—while Army officials said that the survey results are regularly communicated to Army leadership—the surveys are part of a larger ongoing effort that has not been completed, so the results were not available for our review.

[22] Load carriage refers to the equipment and ammunition that individual soldiers carry while undertaking military operations.

[23] The Air Force review identified 7 disqualifying medical conditions that were applicable only to female airmen (including pregnancy), and 10 conditions applicable only to male airmen. It also identified one standard, for anemia, that is enforced differently between males and females due to underlying physiologic differences and baselines.

[24] DOD, memorandum from Under Secretary of Defense for Acquisition, Technology and Logistics, *Guidance on Combat Equipment for Female Military Members* (June 26, 2015). The Carl Levin and Howard P. "Buck" McKeon National Defense Authorization Act for Fiscal Year 2015 § 524(b) (2014) directs the Secretary of Defense to direct the Secretaries of the military departments to ensure that female combat equipment is: (1) properly designed and fitted, and (2) meets required standards for wear and survivability.

[25] These studies are not being conducted by SOCOM, but instead are being conducted by the services' special operations components: Army Special Operations Command, Naval Special Warfare Command, Marine Corps Special Operations Command, and Air Force Special Operations Command.

[26] The Ranger school is currently conducting a one-time assessment of an integrated course to inform its decision on whether to permanently open its Ranger school to women. This assessment is expected to be completed in 2015. If the Ranger special qualification identifier were opened to women, the school would need facility modifications, such as bathrooms and showers, to accommodate women.

[27] The results of these studies are currently for official use only, and thus cannot be disclosed in our report.

[28] The results of this study are currently for official use only, and thus cannot be disclosed in our report.

[29] The Carl Levin and Howard P. "Buck" McKeon National Defense Authorization Act for Fiscal Year 2015, Pub. L. No. 113-291 § 524(c) (2014) included a provision for GAO to review outreach and recruitment efforts focused on representation of women in the officer corps, including identifying and evaluating current initiatives the armed forces are using to increase accession of women into the officer corps. We expect to report on this issue in the fall of 2015.

[30] GAO has recently reported on sexual assaults of male servicemembers. See GAO, *Military Personnel: Actions Needed to Address Sexual Assaults of Male Servicemembers*, GAO-15-284 (Washington, D.C.: Mar. 19, 2015).

[31] Two elements are from statutory requirements, and three elements are from Joint Staff guidance.

[32] As defined by the National Defense Authorization Act for Fiscal Year 1994, Pub. L. No. 103-160 § 543 (1993), as amended by Pub. L. No. 113-66 § 523 (2013), a military career designator refers to, in the case of enlisted members and warrant officers of the armed forces, military occupational specialties, specialty codes, enlisted designators, enlisted classification codes, additional skill identifiers, and special qualification identifiers; and in the case of commissioned officers (other than commissioned warrant officers), officer areas of concentration, occupational specialties, specialty codes, additional skill identifiers, and special qualification identifiers.

[33] National Defense Authorization Act for Fiscal Year 1994, Pub. L. No. 103-160 § 543 (1993), as amended by Pub. L. 113-66 § 523 (2013) (appended as a note below 10 U.S.C. § 113).

[34] Carl Levin and Howard P. "Buck" McKeon National Defense Authorization Act for Fiscal Year 2015, Pub. L. No. 113-291 § 524 (2014).

[35] DOD, memorandum from Under Secretary of Defense for Personnel and Readiness, *Implementation Guidance for Statutory Changes to Occupational Standards* (Mar. 2, 2015), implementing Carl Levin and Howard P. "Buck" McKeon National Defense Authorization Act for Fiscal Year 2015, Pub. L. No. 113-291 § 524 (2014).

[36] These written reports must include a complete listing of all officer and enlisted occupations and the date the occupational standards associated with each were validated; explanation of the methodology used to validate occupational standards, both mental and physical, for

selecting, training, and continuing personnel in each occupation, rating, or specialty; and statements certifying that (1) the occupational standards are gender-neutral, as required by statute; (2) occupational standards meet criteria outlined in statute; accurately predict performance of actual, regular, and recurring duties; and are applied equitably to measure individual capabilities; and (3) validated occupational standards are in use by September 30, 2015, at military occupational specialty schools and training.

[37] These compliance inspections are to be conducted no less frequently than every three years, with the first inspection to be conducted in fiscal year 2016.

[38] *See* DOD, memorandum from the Chairman of the Joint Chiefs of Staff, *Women in the Service Implementation Plan* (Jan. 9, 2013).

[39] According to Marine Corps officials, as of May 2015, for Infantry Training Battalion, 350 women started the training and 136 have graduated; 4,249 men started the training and 4,128 graduated. For Infantry Officer Training, 29 women attempted the course but none graduated. Of the 29 women who attempted the course, 24 of them did not complete the combat endurance test on the first day of training. From fiscal years 2013 through April 17, 2015, 913 men started Infantry Officer Training, and 716 men graduated; of the men who did not graduate, 86 did not complete the combat endurance test.

[40] According to Marine Corps officials, as of May 2015, 75 women joined the Ground Combat Element Integrated Task Force, of which 23 dropped from the study; 284 men joined, of which 117 have dropped from the study. Of the 23 women who dropped, 13 of them dropped for medical reasons; of the 117 men who dropped, 27 dropped for medical reasons.

[41] These studies have varying completion dates, which are discussed earlier.

[42] DOD, memorandum from Secretary of Defense and Chairman of the Joint Chiefs of Staff, *Elimination of the 1994 Direct Ground Combat Definition and Assignment Rule* (Jan. 24, 2013).

[43] GAO, *Standards for Internal Control in the Federal Government*, GAO/AIMD-00-21.3.1 (Washington, D.C.: November 1999).

[44] DOD, memorandum from the Under Secretary of Defense for Personnel and Readiness, *Elimination of the 1994 Direct Ground Combat Definition and Assignment Rule* (Feb. 27, 2013); DOD, memorandum from the Chairman of the Joint Chiefs of Staff, *Women in the Service Implementation Plan* (Jan. 9, 2013).

[45] DOD, memorandum from the Chairman of the Joint Chiefs of Staff, *Women in the Service Implementation Plan* (Jan. 9, 2013). The five guiding principles are: (1) Ensuring the success of the nation's warfighting forces by preserving unit readiness, cohesion, and morale; (2) Ensuring all service men and women are given the opportunity to succeed and are set up for success with viable career paths; (3) Retaining the trust and confidence of the American people to defend this nation by promoting policies that maintain the best quality and most qualified people; (4) Validating both physical and mental occupational performance standards for all military occupational specialties, especially those that remain closed to women; eligibility for training and development within designated occupational fields should consist of qualitative and quantitative standards reflecting the knowledge, skills, and abilities necessary for each occupation; and occupational performance standards for specialties open to women must be gender neutral; (5) Ensuring a sufficient cadre of midgrade/senior enlisted and officers are assigned to commands at the point of introduction to ensure success in the long run; adjust recruiting, assignment processes, and personnel policies if needed; engage in continual in-stride assessments and pilot efforts to inform the assimilation of women into previously closed units.

[46] As discussed earlier, the reporting requirement was changed from quarterly to biannual in July 2014.

[47] RAND's draft report identified as best practices a six-step process for establishing requirements for physically demanding occupations. These six steps are: (1) identify physical demands; (2) identify potential screening tests; (3) validate and select tests; (4)

establish minimum scores; (5) implement screening; and (6) confirm tests are working as intended.

[48] DOD, memorandum from Secretary of Defense and Chairman of the Joint Chiefs of Staff, *Elimination of the 1994 Direct Ground Combat Definition and Assignment Rule* (Jan. 24, 2013).

[49] DOD, memorandum from Secretary of Defense and Chairman of the Joint Chiefs of Staff, *Elimination of the 1994 Direct Ground Combat Definition and Assignment Rule* (Jan. 24, 2013).

[50] GAO/AIMD-00-21.3.1.

[51] DOD, memorandum from Under Secretary of Defense for Personnel and Readiness, *Implementation Guidance for Statutory Changes to Occupational Standards* (Mar. 2, 2015).

[52] 10 U.S.C. § 652.

[53] According to officials, the service Secretary makes a recommendation to open a position or occupation and forwards a package to OUSD(P&R) that details positions and occupations they are requesting to open, verifies the occupational standards, and includes the required detailed analysis of the legal implication of the proposed change with respect to the constitutionality of the application of the Military Selective Service Act (50 U.S.C. App. § 451 et seq.) to males only.

[54] Pub. L. No. 80-759 (1948), as amended (codified as amended at 50 U.S.C. App. § 451 et seq).

[55] 10 U.S.C. § 652.

[56] Section 3 of Pub. L. No. 80-759, codified as amended at 50 U.S.C. App. § 453.

[57] *Rostker v. Goldberg*, 453 U.S. 57 (1981). In this case, the Court found that the purpose of the Selective Service System was to produce a ready group of combat troops, and that, under then-existing law and military guidance, women could not serve in combat. The Court found that the Constitution required that it accord a very high level of deference to Congress' decision, because raising armies is a central function of Congress. The Court also noted that Congress had extensively considered the issue of registering women, finding that the registration of women would not fill a military need because they could not serve as combat troops. The Court therefore found that women were not similarly situated for purposes of the Due Process Clause of the Fifth Amendment to the Constitution with respect to registration under the act, and thus the male-only registration requirement was constitutional.

[58] 10 U.S.C. § 652(a)(1). For purposes of this provision, the continuity of a session of Congress is broken only by an adjournment sine die, which is to say when either house adjourns without a specific date on which they will return. This typically occurs only at the end of each session of Congress.

[59] The OUSD(P&R) 2014 tracking calendar shows that both houses of Congress were in session for 16 days in July, 14 days in March and June, 13 days in January and May, 11 days in February, 10 days in April and December, 8 days in September, 6 days in November, 1 day in August, and 0 days in October.

[60] GAO, *National Security: DOD Should Reevaluate Requirements for the Selective Service System*, GAO-12-623 (Washington, D.C.: June 7, 2012). The Selective Service System is an independent agency in the executive branch. Our report reviewed estimated costs and savings for two alternatives to the current structure of the Selective Service System: (1) placing it in a deep standby mode where active registration is maintained, and (2) disestablishing the agency. In addition to the potential costs and savings of these alternatives, our report also noted that if either alternative were pursued, other factors, with both tangible and intangible costs and benefits, may need to be considered.

[61] Selective Service System, *Annual Report to the Congress of the United States Fiscal Year 2014*.

[62] Memorandum from Assistant Secretary of Defense for Readiness and Force Management, Feb. 26, 2013.

[63] Congressional Research Service, *Women in Combat: Issues for Congress*, CRS R42075 (May 9, 2013), p. 13.

[64] Memorandum from Secretary of Defense and Chairman of the Joint Chiefs of Staff, *Elimination of the 1994 Direct Ground Combat Definition and Assignment Rule* (Jan. 24, 2013).

[65] Memorandum from the Chairman of the Joint Chiefs of Staff, *Women in the Service Implementation Plan* (Jan. 9, 2013).

[66] Memorandum from the Under Secretary of Defense for Personnel and Readiness, *Elimination of the 1994 Direct Ground Combat Definition and Assignment Rule* (Feb. 27, 2013).

[67] Memorandum from the Chairman of the Joint Chiefs of Staff, *Women in the Service Implementation Plan* (Jan. 9, 2013). We found that the military services developed the implementation plans, so we have reviewed those plans based on the requirements provided by the Chairman.

[68] Pub. L. No. 103-160 § 543 (1993), as amended.

[69] Pub. L. No. 113-291 § 524 (2014).

[70] DOD, memorandum from the Chairman of the Joint Chiefs of Staff, *Women in the Service Implementation Plan* (Jan. 9, 2013).

[71] DOD, memorandum from the Secretary of Defense and Chairman of the Joint Chiefs of Staff, *Elimination of the 1994 Direct Ground Combat Definition and Assignment Rule* (Jan. 24, 2013); and memorandum from the Chairman of the Joint Chiefs of Staff, *Women in the Service Implementation Plan* (Jan. 9, 2013).

[72] GAO, *Standards for Internal Control in the Federal Government*, GAO/AIMD-00-21.3.1 (Washington, D.C.: Nov. 1999).

[73] 10 U.S.C. § 652.

[74] Pub. L. No. 80-759 (1948), as amended (codified at 50 U.S.C. App. § 451 et seq).

[75] See S. Rep. No. 96-226 (1979); S. Rep. No. 96-826 (1980); S. Conf. Rep. No. 96-895 (1980); 126 Cong. Rec. 8601-8602, 8620 (1980); H. J. Res. No. 521 (1980).

[76] *Rostker v. Goldberg*, 453 U.S. 57 (1981).

[77] See, for example, GAO, *National Security: DOD Should Reevaluate Requirements for the Selective Service System*, GAO-12-623 (Washington, D.C.: June 7, 2012); GAO, *Women in the Military: Impact of Proposed Legislation to Open More Combat Support Positions and Units to Women*, GAO/NSIAD-88-197BR (Washington, D.C.: July 15, 1988).

[78] Congressional Research Service, *Women in Combat: Issues for Congress*, CRS R42075 (May 9, 2013).

[79] Defense Advisory Committee on Women in the Services, December 4-5, 2014 quarterly meeting minutes.

In: Combat Service Opportunities for Women ISBN: 978-1-63484-432-1
Editor: Cassandra Schultz

Chapter 3

MEMORANDUM RE: WOMEN IN THE SERVICE IMPLEMENTATION PLAN*

General Martin E. Dempsey

INFO MEMO

FOR: SECRETARY OF DEFENSE FROM: General Martin E. Dempsey, CJCS
SUBJECT: Women in the Service Implementation Plan

The time has come to rescind the direct combat exclusion rule for women and to eliminate all unnecessary gender-based barriers to service. The Joint Chiefs of Staff unanimously join me in proposing that we move forward with the full intent to integrate women into occupational fields to the maximum extent possible. To implement these initiatives successfully and without sacrificing our warfighting capability or the trust of the American people, we will need time to get it right.

- We recognize the bravery and contributions of women in combat. We have made tremendous progress in expanding service opportunities for women since your February 2012 announcement, which officially

* This is an edited, reformatted and augmented version of a memorandum from the Chairman of the Joint Chiefs of Staff, issued January 9, 2013.

notified Congress of the Department's intent to rescind the co-location restriction and to implement Exceptions to Policy (ETP) allowing women to be assigned to select positions in ground combat units at the battalion level. Recently, the Services opened 13,139 positions under co-location and an additional 1,186 positions under Exceptions to Policy.

- *Guiding Principles.* To successfully integrate women into the remaining restricted occupational fields within our military, we must keep our guiding principles at the forefront We are driven by:
  - Ensuring the success of our Nation's warfighting forces by preserving unit readiness, cohesion, and morale.
  - Ensuring all Service men and women are given the opportunity to succeed and are set up for success with viable career paths.
  - Retaining the trust and confidence of the American people to defend this Nation by promoting policies that maintain the best quality and most qualified people.
  - Validating occupational performance standards, both physical and mental, for all military occupational specialties (MOSs), specifically those that remain closed to women. Eligibility for training and development within designated occupational fields should consist of qualitative and quantifiable standards reflecting the knowledge, skills, and abilities necessary for each occupation. For occupational specialties open to women, the occupational performance standards must be gender-neutral as required by Public Law 103-160, Section 542 (1993).
  - Ensuring that a sufficient cadre of midgrade/senior women enlisted and officers are assigned to commands at the point of introduction to ensure success in the long run. This may require an adjustment to our recruiting efforts, assignment processes, and personnel policies. Assimilation of women into heretofore "closed units" will be informed by continual in-stride assessments and pilot efforts.
- Goals and Milestones. The following goals and milestones will support the elimination of unnecessary gender-based barriers to service:
  - Services will expand the number of units and number of women assigned to those units—based on ETP—and provide periodic updates on progress each quarter beginning in 3rd quarter, FY 2013.

  - The Navy will continue to assign women to afloat units as: (1) technical changes and modifications for reasonable female privacy and appropriate female berthing arrangements are completed; (2) female officer and enlisted leadership assignments can be implemented; and (3) ships' schedules permit. Integration will be expeditiously implemented considering good order and judicious use of fiscal resources.
  - Services will continue to develop, review, and validate individual occupational standards. Validated gender-neutral occupational standards will be used to assess and assign Service members not later than September 2015.
  - The Services and U.S. Special Operations Command (USSOCOM) will proceed in a deliberate, measured and responsible way to assign women to currently closed MOSs as physical standards and operational assessments are completed and as it becomes possible to introduce cadres as described above. The Services and USSOCOM must complete all studies by 1st quarter, FY 2016, and provide periodic updates each quarter beginning in 3rd quarter, FY 2013.
  - If we find that the assignment of women to a specific position or occupational specialty is in conflict with our stated principles, we will request an exception to policy.
- This deliberate approach to reducing gender-based barriers to women's service will provide the time necessary to institutionalize these important changes and to integrate women into occupational fields in a climate where they can succeed and flourish. Ultimately, we will ensure the success of our military forces and maintain the trust of the American people.

In: Combat Service Opportunities for Women ISBN: 978-1-63484-432-1
Editor: Cassandra Schultz

Chapter 4

MEMORANDUM RE: ELIMINATION OF THE 1994 DIRECT GROUND COMBAT DEFINITION AND ASSIGNMENT RULE*

General Martin E. Dempsey and Leon E. Panetta

We are fully committed to removing as many barriers as possible to joining, advancing, and succeeding in the U.S. Armed Forces. Success in our military based solely on ability, qualifications, and performance is consistent with our values and enhances military readiness. Today, women make up 15% of the U.S. military and are indispensable to the national security mission. In fact, thousands of women have served alongside men in Iraq and Afghanistan, and like men, have been exposed to hostile enemy action in those countries. However, many positions in our military remain closed to women because of the 1994 Direct Ground Combat Definition and Assignment Rule.

In February 2012, in collaboration with the Joint Chiefs of Staff, we modified the 1994 Rule, thereby opening up over 14,000 positions previously closed to women. Subsequently, the Joint Chiefs of Staff reviewed the 1994 Direct Ground Combat Definition and Assignment Rule and they now propose a way forward that will fully integrate women without compromising our readiness, morale, or war-fighting capacity. We agree with their approach and

---

* This is an edited, reformatted and augmented version of a memorandum from the Chairman of the Joint Chiefs of Staff and the Secretary of Defense, issued January 24, 2013.

guiding principles, and the milestones they propose. A copy of the memorandum explaining the advice of the Joint Chiefs of Staff is attached.

Therefore, the 1994 Direct Ground Combat Definition and Assignment Rule excluding women from assignment to units and positions whose primary mission is to engage in direct combat on the ground is rescinded effective immediately. Currently closed units and positions will be opened by each relevant Service, consistent with the guiding principles set forth in the attached memorandum and after the development and implementation of validated, gender-neutral occupational standards and the required notifications to Congress. The Military Departments shall submit by May 15, 2013, to the Secretary of Defense through the Chairman of the Joint Chiefs of Staff and the Under Secretary of Defense for Personnel and Readiness, their detailed plans for the implementation of this directive. Their plans shall be consistent with the guiding principles, and goals and milestones contained in the attached memorandum.

Integration of women into newly opened positions and units will occur as expeditiously as possible, considering good order and judicious use of fiscal resources, but must be completed no later than January 1, 2016. Any recommendation to keep an occupational specialty or unit closed to women must be personally approved first by the Chairman of the Joint Chiefs of Staff, and then by the Secretary of Defense; this approval authority may not be delegated. Exceptions must be narrowly tailored, and based on a rigorous analysis of factual data regarding the knowledge, skills and abilities needed for the position. The Military Departments shall submit quarterly progress reports on their implementation of this memo to the Secretary of Defense through the Chairman of the Joint Chiefs of Staff and the Under Secretary of Defense for Personnel and Readiness.

Martin E. Dempsey General, USA
Chairman of the Joint Chiefs of aff

Leon E. Panetta
Secretary of Defense

Attachment: As stated
cc:
Under Secretary of Defense for Acquisition, Technology, and Logistics
Under Secretary of Defense for Policy
Under Secretary of Defense for Intelligence

General Counsel of the Department of Defense
Assistant Secretary of Defense for Legislative Affairs
Assistant Secretary of Defense for Public Affairs

INDEX

#

21st century, 10

A

access, 7, 23
accessions, 13
accommodations, 51
accountability, 13, 54
adaptation(s), 25, 52, 76
adjustment, 16, 88
advancement, 24, 30
advocacy, 7, 23
Afghanistan, 2, 10, 35, 38, 91
age, 5, 19, 27, 29
agencies, 69
Air Force, 3, 8, 14, 15, 16, 28, 29, 31, 37, 42, 43, 44, 46, 47, 49, 51, 52, 55, 57, 58, 69, 78, 79, 80, 81, 82, 83
American Red Cross, 5
amphibia, 76
anemia, 83
armed forces, vii, 1, 5, 6, 7, 40, 65, 83
assault, 20, 30, 43, 54, 72, 76
assessment, 14, 19, 20, 21, 37, 61, 67, 75, 83
assimilation, 84
attitudes, 50
audit, 39, 74
authority, 4, 17, 24, 26, 29, 54, 62, 92

B

Barbados, 6
barriers, 3, 13, 15, 19, 25, 28, 50, 61, 76, 78, 87, 88, 89, 91
benefits, 78, 85

C

campaigns, 53
candidates, 14
case law, 73
challenges, vii, 22, 35, 36, 39, 43, 50, 54, 59, 66, 70, 71
Chief of Staff, 21
citizens, 6
civil rights, 7
clarity, 6
classes, 36, 45, 47, 52, 62, 73
classification, 83
climate, 25, 89
clothing, 52
CNN, 31
Coast Guard, 5, 29, 31, 69
collaboration, 63, 91
communication, 60
community(s), 17, 53, 77, 79
compliance, 11, 57, 84

composition, 52
conflict, vii, 1, 2, 7, 21, 89
Congress, vii, 1, 2, 4, 5, 6, 8, 9, 11, 12, 13, 14, 15, 17, 18, 19, 23, 24, 25, 26, 27, 28, 29, 30, 31, 40, 42, 44, 47, 49, 65, 66, 67, 68, 71, 82, 85, 86, 88, 92
consent, 27
Constitution, 29, 85
contingency, 38
coordination, 14, 46, 60
cost, 9, 12, 20, 22, 53, 66
counterterrorism, 81
cycles, 66

D

data collection, 77
decision makers, 64, 68
decoration, 28
Department of Defense, vii, 1, 2, 6, 28, 29, 30, 31, 32, 37, 38, 42, 44, 69, 81, 93
differential treatment, 6
direct action, 32
diversity, 12, 13
draft, 5, 6, 23, 24, 61, 65, 66, 67, 68, 84

E

endurance, 18, 19, 56, 84
environment(s), 2, 10, 13, 20, 25, 32, 37, 51, 58, 66, 67, 73, 75
equal opportunity, 2, 4, 5, 17, 23
equipment, 43, 50, 52, 72, 82, 83
ethnic minority, 14
ethnicity, 13, 28
evacuation, 6, 20
evidence, 11, 20, 25, 40, 74
exclusion, 2, 8, 11, 13, 14, 15, 27, 66, 76, 87
executive branch, 85
exposure, 7, 27

F

Federal Government, 60, 63, 84, 86
Fifth Amendment, 85
fiscal year, 44, 53, 59, 60, 66, 70, 84
fitness, 19, 42
flexibility, 15
flight, 7, 29
focus groups, 51, 75, 77
force, 5, 7, 9, 17, 25, 44, 45, 51, 71, 75, 81, 82

G

General Accounting Office (GAO), 7, 30, 35, 36, 37, 38, 41, 42, 44, 45, 46, 48, 49, 55, 69, 71, 73, 79, 80, 81, 83, 84, 85, 86
Germany, 29
Grenada, 6, 29
group membership, 82
Guam, 29
guidance, 36, 37, 39, 52, 56, 57, 60, 62, 63, 66, 67, 70, 72, 73, 82, 83, 85
guiding principles, 43, 51, 57, 58, 61, 70, 72, 84, 88, 92

H

harassment, 43, 54
health, 19, 36, 42, 43, 50, 51, 71
health effects, 51
health problems, 51
history, 2, 4, 25, 29, 73
homogeneity, 25
homosexuals, 25
House, 9, 11, 12, 30, 38, 65
House of Representatives, 38
Hunter, 2, 12

I

identification, 13, 70
individuals, 19, 25, 58
injury(s), 4, 10, 20, 22, 30, 51, 52, 77
injury prevention, 51, 77
inspections, 84
insurance policy, 66

integration, vii, 3, 17, 22, 25, 36, 37, 38, 39, 43, 45, 50, 51, 52, 53, 54, 59, 60, 61, 64, 67, 68, 73, 75, 76, 77, 78, 81
intelligence, 45
intervention, 6
Iraq, 2, 7, 10, 30, 35, 38, 91
issues, vii, 1, 2, 4, 9, 12, 17, 27, 28, 32, 38, 43, 50, 51, 53, 61, 71, 75

J

justification, 23, 40, 81

K

Kuwait, 7

L

laws, 8, 14, 17, 24, 40, 72
leadership, 13, 14, 23, 24, 25, 54, 77, 82, 89
legislation, 5, 29
life cycle, 13
light, 32, 37, 66, 67
living arrangements, 30
logistics, 77

M

majority, 10, 24, 40, 46
management, 60
manpower, 2, 4, 17
Marine Corps, 3, 5, 10, 15, 17, 19, 20, 21, 25, 26, 28, 31, 32, 33, 37, 41, 42, 44, 45, 46, 47, 50, 51, 52, 53, 56, 57, 58, 59, 64, 69, 75, 76, 77, 79, 81, 83, 84
materials, 54
matter, 2, 57, 59
McCain, Senator John, 38
medical, 4, 7, 51, 83, 84
medical reason, 84
mental health, 51
methodology, 39, 72, 83
military, vii, 1, 2, 3, 4, 5, 6, 8, 11, 13, 14, 15, 16, 17, 18, 19, 20, 21, 22, 23, 24, 25, 26, 27, 28, 35, 36, 37, 38, 39, 40, 42, 43, 45, 46, 47, 49, 51, 52, 53, 56, 57, 60, 61, 63, 64, 65, 66, 67, 69, 70, 72, 73, 74, 75, 77, 81, 82, 83, 84, 85, 86, 88, 89, 91
military occupation, 2, 3, 16, 19, 20, 57, 75, 77, 83, 84, 88
minorities, 14
minority groups, 25
mission(s), vii, 1, 5, 6, 7, 8, 9, 10, 11, 15, 27, 31, 32, 40, 59, 67, 78, 81, 82, 91, 92
modifications, 12, 17, 47, 83, 89
morale, 16, 22, 25, 59, 72, 77, 84, 88, 91
musculoskeletal, 22
museums, 29

N

National Defense Authorization Act, 2, 9, 11, 12, 18, 19, 32, 38, 55, 72, 81, 82, 83
national emergency, 24
national security, 23, 25, 66, 67, 91
neutral, vii, 2, 9, 15, 16, 17, 18, 20, 23, 27, 28, 35, 36, 39, 42, 51, 56, 57, 58, 60, 61, 70, 72, 73, 78, 79, 84, 88, 89, 92
nurses, 29

O

obstacles, 37, 50, 64, 68, 78
officials, 12, 36, 39, 45, 47, 50, 51, 52, 53, 54, 56, 58, 59, 61, 62, 63, 64, 65, 66, 67, 70, 71, 72, 73, 82, 84, 85
Operation Enduring Freedom, 3, 10, 28
Operation Iraqi Freedom, 3, 10, 28
operations, vii, 1, 3, 6, 8, 9, 11, 22, 30, 32, 38, 40, 44, 45, 47, 50, 52, 58, 59, 60, 62, 63, 78, 81, 82, 83
opportunities, 2, 5, 10, 13, 14, 15, 24, 28, 30, 40, 45, 68, 69, 73, 87
outreach, 53, 83
oversight, vii, 2, 17, 36, 37, 39, 54, 60, 61, 63, 67, 73

P

parental consent, 5, 27
participants, 77
peer review, 79
Pentagon, 12, 31, 32
permit, 24, 89
Persian Gulf, 80
Persian Gulf War, 80
Philippines, 29
physical fitness, 19, 42, 52
platform, 9
playing, 13
police, 6
policy, vii, 1, 2, 3, 4, 6, 7, 8, 9, 10, 11, 12, 14, 15, 16, 27, 30, 31, 32, 36, 39, 41, 42, 43, 47, 60, 62, 63, 70, 73, 82, 89
pregnancy, 83
President, 29, 30, 31, 65
prevention, 54
principles, 16, 70, 89, 92
prisoners, 5
prisoners of war, 5
probability, 9, 82
professional development, 62
programming, 81
progress reports, 37, 39, 44, 60, 61, 64, 70, 71, 73, 82, 92
psychological health, 76
public concern, 7

Q

qualifications, 18, 91

R

race, 13
racial minorities, 25
reasoning, 66
recommendations, 2, 6, 7, 9, 12, 13, 17, 39, 41, 45, 49, 53, 63, 64, 67, 70
recovery, 32
recruiting, 3, 5, 16, 22, 45, 53, 66, 84, 88
Reform, 30
registration laws, 24
regulations, 9, 14, 18, 40
Rehnquist, William, 24
relevance, 15, 41
reliability, 39, 71
Reorganization Act, 4, 26
requirement(s), vii, 2, 5, 8, 10, 15, 18, 19, 20, 21, 27, 35, 36, 37, 39, 40, 42, 53, 56, 57, 58, 59, 64, 65, 66, 67, 68, 70, 72, 73, 83, 84, 85, 86
resistance, 25
resolution, 29
resource availability, 20
resources, 47, 81, 89, 92
response, 7, 43, 53, 54, 79
restrictions, 3, 6, 9, 24, 40, 81
rights, 3, 5, 23
risk(s), 7, 8, 9, 10, 20, 22, 27, 51
risk factors, 51

S

savings, 85
school, 21, 52, 58, 83, 84
scope, 39, 69, 72
Secretary of Defense, vii, 1, 3, 6, 8, 9, 11, 12, 14, 16, 17, 18, 23, 26, 28, 31, 35, 38, 39, 40, 43, 44, 47, 49, 52, 57, 60, 61, 62, 63, 65, 66, 67, 68, 69, 70, 74, 81, 82, 83, 84, 85, 86, 91, 92, 93
security, 81
Senate, 6, 9, 14, 29, 35, 38, 65, 81
services, vii, 4, 5, 7, 8, 10, 15, 20, 21, 23, 24, 25, 28, 35, 36, 37, 38, 39, 40, 42, 43, 44, 45, 47, 50, 52, 53, 54, 56, 57, 58, 59, 60, 61, 62, 63, 64, 65, 66, 67, 68, 69, 70, 71, 72, 73, 74, 81, 82, 83, 86
sex, 54
sexual assaults, 54, 83
sexual harassment, 71
shape, 64
shock, 9, 82
simulations, 59
society, 23

states, 31, 56, 60, 62, 63
statutes, 5, 36, 37, 67, 72, 73
structure, 17, 37, 66, 67, 71, 85
submarines, 8, 12, 27, 28
Supreme Court, 24, 65, 73
sustainability, 77
synchronize, 46

T

tactics, 81
talent, 32
Task Force, 6, 20, 29, 56, 57, 58, 69, 75, 76, 77, 79, 84
teams, 20, 78
technical change, 89
technical comments, 68
tempo, 15
testing, 19, 21, 58
threats, 37, 67
training, 5, 10, 12, 16, 21, 22, 32, 51, 52, 58, 64, 66, 75, 77, 78, 81, 82, 84, 88
transport, 29

U

United Kingdom, 22, 32
United States, 3, 5, 29, 35, 38, 85
USA, 92

V

validation, 17, 20, 22, 28, 36, 45, 56, 57, 58, 59, 60, 61, 62, 64, 74, 75, 78
vehicles, 52
vessels, vii, 1, 5, 7, 8, 9, 26, 27, 32
Volunteers, 76

W

waiver, 32
war, 5, 24, 29, 91
War on Terror, 3
Washington, 4, 29, 30, 31, 32, 80, 81, 83, 84, 85, 86
weapons, 4, 9, 10, 20, 23, 81, 82
weapons of mass destruction, 81
wear, 22, 52, 83
workforce, 73
World War I, 4, 5, 7, 11